12 AGONAL BREATHS

A STORY ABOUT A WOMAN WHO TAUGHT ME HOW TO BREATHE

AL & YVETTE ROWLETT

outskirtspress

DENVER, COLORADO

Contents

Dedication

This book is dedicated to my Lord and Savior, Jesus Christ, without whom this would not have been possible. To my late wife Yvette T. Rowlett, I love you and thank you for our 28 years together. To my children, Kyaime, LaTyia, Kimberly, Kirkland, Tyler, Trey, Culese, and Hannah, my grandchildren, Bible-study sisters, Honor-Bound brothers, family, and friends: this manuscript is for all of you.

A special thanks to Joy Atienza, Erin Jefferson, and Alexis Bernard, who were unfailingly supportive and kind.

Very Special thanks to Bruce Robinson Photography for the magnificent photographs.

Preface

By definition, "agonal breathing" is an abnormal pattern of respiration characterized by shallow, slow (3–4 per minute), irregular inspirations followed by irregular pauses.

On Saturday, December 5, 2009, at 12:00 a.m., I was reporting for my graveyard shift at the hospital. As the graveyard shift was beginning, I telephoned the regularly scheduled worker to inform her that I would be working so she could take the shift off. She did not answer or get my message; consequently, she arrived shortly after my call. She was wearing an elaborate outfit that would have made Lady Gaga proud. I stared, at first, as the reflection from the sequins was blinding. Clearly, she had been at an event before arriving here, but she was here now, ready for her shift. I told her I was going to work 1:1 with my favorite patient that night. She acquiesced. Yes! I know you are not supposed to get attached to your patients, but I felt a particular fondness for this one. I really wanted to work that shift.

The next morning, December 5th, 7 a.m., I left, though reluctantly, because something about my favorite patient seemed different. I had decided she was going to get better. Denial had pursued me all night, and by morning I was fully embracing it. Her friends, "the Bible-study sisters," wanted to visit with her early on Saturday morning. They showed up—two of them anyway—as I had other responsibilities (though less important than my shifts at the hospital) that needed attending to. So I unwillingly left the patient with them and decided to go and assess my Saturday crew's progress, since they were preparing for the training on Monday. That same morning, around 9:30 a.m., my daughters telephoned to ask me to come home in order to wash and blow-dry Hannah's (their baby sister's) hair. After listening to their cajoling, I reluctantly agreed. I was needed everywhere, it seemed. I had wanted to revisit the patient, but I was reminded that adequate staffing was already in place until I returned for the graveyard shift on Sunday.

When I arrived at the office I worked nervously for about thirty minutes, then I realized I was fatigued from the activity associated with caring for the patient. I made a few sarcastic jokes, and tried to stay focused on the task at hand, but my heart and mind were elsewhere. I was still having trouble concentrating when I received an urgent call on my cellular phone. I made a brief statement to my staff, excusing myself before heading back to the hospital.

I reluctantly chose to drive directly to the hospital, rationalizing that Hannah's hair and the training would take care of themselves. When I arrived at the hospital, I got on the elevator and pushed the button that corresponded with the fourth floor. I remember exiting the elevator and gazing around as the nurses and doctors looked at me; they were pleasant but watchful as I walked into the patient's room.

It was approximately 11:00 a.m. I gazed at my favorite patient. I wondered when I would see her get up, or if a stay at an intermediate care facility was in order. I refused to accept that she was dying. She was only 51 years old; how could this be happening? I shut the door to her room and watched her breathe. Her rapid breathing caused her chest to rise and fall, like the pistons on an engine that I had once seen in a documentary. By this time, denial had released its hold on me. I sat down in a chair and prayed, "God, if you are not going to restore her flesh, please take her home."

I was tired and confused, but I heard it, a "still small voice" say, "… if you are going to pray that type of prayer, servant, get on your knees."

I tentatively got on my knees and repeated the same prayer: "God, if you are not going to restore her flesh, take her home." A minute or two had passed, as I stood watchfully over her bed, when I heard the "still small voice" again, urging me to make a telephone call. I telephoned the graveyard shift worker and within 30 seconds she opened the door and greeted me, still adorned in sequins.

"What's going on? I'm here!"

I was perplexed; I thought she had taken the night off.

She said, "I was at the hospital. When you said you did not need me, I spent the night in the hospital lounge and slept on the couch."

That explained why she was still wearing her extravagant outfit. As for why she had stayed at all, well, this was a devoted graveyard worker. The two of us waited with the patient. Again, I heard the "still small voice."

This time the voice said, "Call her mother!"

Call her mother? I was exhausted and anxious; I did not want to do anything. *Why?* I thought, confused as I telephoned her mother.

She answered, and after a brief discussion said, "I will be up there to visit at 3:00 p.m. or so."

I replied, "I think something is different."

After a momentary pause, she said, "I am on my way. I'll be right there!"

Less than thirty minutes after our conversation, the patient's mother entered the room. The three of us just stood as the patient lay there on the bed. Three of us stood around the patient's bed like mother hens watching chicks. A few minutes passed. A nurse came into the room and gave the patient some medication for pain. She placed the syringe with medication in the IV and left. Shortly after that, we all noticed something. It was sudden, but we all noticed it: we could hear her breath. She was breathing! They were desperate breaths. I had never heard breathing like that; that beautiful young lady, our beloved patient, started to breathe. Then suddenly, remarkably, she removed the oxygen mask from her face. We were shocked. Her mother and I in an instant tried to put it back on.

She resisted, almost violently, and then a miracle happened: for the first time in over a day she spoke, "No!"

It was the weakest, most beautiful "no" I had ever heard. "*No!*"

I looked at her as her mother continued the struggle to try to put the mask back on her face. My arms went limp.

I looked at the patient's eyes; she said it again, "No!"

She looked at me and I spoke words that I never thought I would ever speak. "Stop! Leave her alone." The struggle was over.

Then there was sound like the wind stirring leaves; it was an unmistakable sound. **A beautiful, strong woman of God—a wife, mother, sister, and daughter—was going home.** This story is a partial account of her life prior to those final **12 Agonal Breaths**.

Introduction

In Her Own Words

Why write? Why are we writing this? If her story will encourage someone going through a storm to hold their head up and keep trying, then it is worth writing. If this will help someone to see past the storm until the sun comes up, then it is worth writing. The Bible tells us that "... tomorrow is not promised" to any of us, and that we should live our lives knowing that if we die today, everything is going to be all right. Most of us never want to think about death and dying. We want to live today and plan for tomorrow. She was no different. She planned for tomorrow and next week and even months from now, but she always tried to live knowing that if she was not here tomorrow, it was going to be okay.

She had dreams and plans and desires. She wanted to support her husband in all that he did. She wanted to go to church. She wanted to be here to influence her children, grandchildren, and other family members. She wanted to go to soccer games and dance recitals. She wanted to shop, eat out, swim, and read yet another good book. There was so much she wanted to do.

She wanted to go to the continent of Africa again and work with the people in the country of Zambia, bettering their lives and the lives of their children. She had such a heart for the poor and desolate. Yes, she had her own battles to fight, but she would assert, "…The battles don't seem so big when you focus on someone else. I have a wonderful husband, a beautiful home, a supportive family, great friends, bosom buddies, a job I love, and so much more to be thankful for. Some people have no hope. These days, I cannot fathom what that might feel like. I do remember when I was younger and would sometimes feel like there was no hope, but God always brought someone across my path to encourage me and let me know He loves me. As long as God loved me, I had hope. For some people, life has just beaten them down. Sometimes it's family issues, drugs, alcohol, lack of education or a good job; whatever it is, I know some people have no hope. I say to you, *'Look at me! A skinny little black girl from the East Coast with all the makings of a failure.'* God has picked me up, dusted me off, and blessed me more than I could have ever imagined.

"I still have issues, I still have family members who are not living for the Lord and are really struggling with life. I have family members that are so stricken with anger and bitterness that they have no peace. They have not turned to the Lord, maybe because of hurt they experienced in the church. Whatever the reason, they are hurting and it makes me hurt. I love people and I know the peace that God can give us. I want to stand on top of a mountain and yell down for people to pay attention and give God a chance."

She lived her life for God, but she was adamant and defiant about the way life should be lived for Him. "Some people think that if you live for the Lord you have to go to church all the time, not have any kind of fun, stop doing anything social or entertaining, and stay at home reading your Bible all the time. That is such a lie! Christians have so much fun."

Life was an exciting adventure for her, enhanced by her faith and love. It was especially fun when she first got married; they were a young Christian couple starting to explore the Word of God. She would read something in the Bible and would say, "OK, Lord, show me!" She wanted God to prove His word to her. She would make a commitment to do something and then wait for God to do what His word says.

Her examples taught people so much through that process. She would often remind her husband, "God really wants to meet us right where we are and carry us forward. He means good for us, even though we don't always know what the end result is going to be. Let's give Him a chance, and I guarantee you will not regret it."

She was at times unorthodox. She told a story about a day when her girlfriend, Renita, saw a hairstyle that they liked and wanted to try. She liked to braid hair, and was willing to try almost any new hairstyle. So, off to the store they went to buy the tools they needed for the particular braids.

"We thought we would see a picture of it, and we could figure it out from there, if we had directions. Well, we get in the store and there is nothing. My mother was with us and she was laughing at us, saying we were always coming up with something silly. So, Renita and I decided that if we needed an answer, that we should pray and ask the Lord for what we needed to create these braids. We looked at each other and agreed that the Word says if two or more are gathered in His name, He would be there. There were three of us! Although, we weren't sure Mother was on board with this request. No problem, two was good enough. Sounded like the best solution we had."

She would often tell people that right there in the aisle of that store they held hands and started praying for God to tell them what tool to buy. She said her mother was shocked. According to her, when they stopped praying, her mother said, "…You two are worrying the Lord about a braiding tool when people have real issues that they need to talk to the Lord about! Leave the Lord alone and go ask a real beautician how to fix the braids." They were unabashed. "We laughed so hard! We were very serious about asking the Lord. He knows everything, and this was important to us, so why not? Well, we got a regular knitting needle and knit us some braids in our hair. It worked perfectly. I don't know if that's what the 'real beauticians' used, but it worked for us. I believe the Lord gave us the wisdom to buy it." She believed that when you sincerely ask the Lord for something, He answers. She was fond of saying, "Come on! He knows everything!"

She was thankful that God allowed her to be an instrument to be used by Him. In December of 2009, she said, "I asked the Lord to allow me to touch His people. I believe in this short life of mine, He has allowed me to touch His people and I have been touched by His people. So, share my story with them. I am hoping that it will touch someone's heart, because I know that if this skinny little black girl can make a difference, so can they. God needs us to love ourselves and love one another. He can take it from there."

Her Prayer

"Dear Lord,

Thank you for allowing me to live this long. Thank you for loving me more than I love myself, and for teaching me to love others. I pray that what I write will encourage others to keep up a good fight, to look beyond the sad times, and know that the sun will rise. Lord, thank you for being the sun in my life; thank you for giving me hope when I had none and for giving me years of laughter and adventure.

"I thank you for today and for tomorrow. I believe I have more adventures to live and ask for wisdom as I try to live this life for You. Thank you for the people I encounter on my job. I love them and take seriously any time that I have with them. Help me to focus on one person at a time and be engaged in their life for that moment, hour, or day.

"I pray that my family members will read this and be encouraged. That they will appreciate the past and look forward to the future in a new way; if they are not living for You, Lord, I pray that You will draw them to You and bring others across their paths to encourage them and remind them that You love them.

"I pray. This is written from my heart; I am not holding back. Help me to be sensitive to what You would have me to share. Oh Lord, I pray that this work would be pleasing to You. Your servant, Yvette Twana Rowlett. In Jesus' Name, Amen."

1

The Early Years: Through the Storm

She was born Yvette Twanna Peters. She would describe growing up this way: "My childhood was full of ups and downs. I had the best of the best sometimes, and sometimes I also experienced losses that no child should experience. I was born to James and Ida, who were married for about eight years and had three other children. My oldest brother, Tyrone, was my father's child and two years old when they married. Together they had my brother Jimmy in 1956, my sister Pamela 10 months later, and then me 18 months after Pamela.

"They met in Washington, DC, where my father was born and raised, and we lived there until I was about two years old. My father was a young Baptist minister and my mother stayed home and cared for the family. My father was called to a church in Bridgeport, Connecticut. Life was great as far as I was concerned.

"My parents were involved in the Civil Rights Movement. My father worked closely with Dr. Martin Luther King, Jr., and other great civil rights activists. As a result, my father was well known in Bridgeport, and soon throughout the East Coast.

"On Thanksgiving Day, during my kindergarten year in school, my parents got into a big fight and my father left home. He never came back. At the time, we lived in a very nice suburban home, but that would change. Eventually, we had to move out, my mother had to find a job, and we would learn what the term 'latchkey kid' meant.

"We stopped attending the church my father pastored, and the bitter battle for custody would begin soon after. Church members were torn; some would visit us and others wouldn't even speak if they saw us in public. I was confused.

"I remember that my oldest brother left that fateful Thanksgiving Day with my father and never lived with us again. Now, it was my mom, my brother, my sister, and I. We had to move. We ended up moving into the public-housing projects. My mother and brother don't like elevators; we lived on the second floor so they could walk up the stairs. One thing I remember about the projects was the elevator. It would always smell like urine. It was not safe, but neither were the stairs. No matter which way you chose, the rule was: go quickly, and do not go alone.

"We started attending the local public school, and most kids knew who we were. They teased us a lot, as we were the pastor's kids who used to be 'rich' and now had nothing. After my sister was in a few fights (I always seemed to avoid them), my mother decided she couldn't leave us in that school.

"We transferred to a Catholic school. Why Catholic school, when we used to be Baptist? Who knows! Some say the Catholic schools were the best educationally, others say it was to get back at my very popular Baptist father. Either way, I was in third grade when I was enrolled at St. Charles Parochial School. The school was on the other side of town and we had to catch two, sometimes three, buses to get there. I remember my mother would drop us off at school in the morning, but the bus ride home in the evening took several hours. There were three African American kids attending the school that year: my brother, my sister, and myself. Wow, talk about culture change! We knew nothing about being Catholic, and I rebelled against any attempt to teach me Catholicism. I was Baptist and I wanted everyone to know it. The next year, I remember another African American family enrolled their two sons. We became an anti-Catholic gang; we also all became good friends.

"In fourth grade, I had Sister Mary Magdala as my teacher. She was not nice at all. But now, when I look back on my circumstance, I'm sure she was praying for me daily and asking the Lord for direction regarding what she should do for me. Sister Magdala and I went through a lot. I don't think she really wanted me there, and I surely didn't want to be there.

"I did everything I could to prove to her I was black and proud and that I would never act like my white counterparts. One day, my mother had my sister and I wear some afro wigs to school. They were so big! There was no way the students sitting behind us could see over or around them. It was the '70s and that was the style. Sister Magdala asked me to take it off and of course I refused. When she attempted to take it off of me, I remembered what my mother said: 'You better not let anybody take it off your head!' I didn't let her: that may not have been my first trip to the principal's office, but it was the most memorable. There were many more conversations with the principal; they always ended with calling my mother.

"Unfortunately, the school figured it was easier to deal with us kids than to call my mother and bother her with the school issues. I remember one day they called my father. My mother had not put him on the list of people to call. Boy, did they get a piece of my mother's mind that day! That was how my father found out what school we attended. It was terrible.

"In fifth grade, we were transferred to St. Ambrose, where there were more African American kids. Things were different and, yes, I missed Sister Magdala. At least she cared; here they just left us alone. In sixth grade, my sister and I were sent to Gainsville, Virginia, to live with a friend of my mother. There were eight kids in the house. A grandmother, mother, and her kids all lived there. It was in the country, so we had to do some adjusting. The kids would make fun of our accent, which we thought was funny because they were the ones with the country accents, but we wouldn't dare say it aloud.

"My sister and I were assigned to different schools. My sister went to middle school; I was still in elementary. The other kids were all in high school, except one daughter who was in sixth grade with me. It was a great year. I had breakfast, lunch, and dinner every day; that was a first. Aunt Kay could cook and I enjoyed her food. There was always someone home to look after us. We were never on our own.

"We were told not to contact my father, so he didn't know where we were. I believe it was his year to have custody of my sister and I, and my mother was opposed to that. Yes, we were in hiding, but we didn't quite understand what that meant. My sister and I understood that we could not contact Daddy. That was fine with me as long as things were going well. One day, however, I was not happy about something and decided I was ready to go back to Connecticut. I wrote my father a letter and had a friend from school mail it.

"The next thing I knew, the police and several cars were speeding down the driveway. It was my dad with his backup. I was so scared he was going to tell on me for writing that letter. After some discussion, it was determined that we were not in danger and it would be best if we stayed, finished the school year, and then went to visit him. I was glad to see Daddy, but deep down I did not want to live with him. I liked Aunt Kay and the fact that I could rest at night and not worry about anything. I knew this was what a family was supposed to be like.

"In seventh grade I was back in Bridgeport, Connecticut. My mother was living in Trumbull, Connecticut, and caring for an elderly man, Max. We had a home in Bridgeport, but went to school in Trumbull, where the wealthier families lived. It was a better school. That would not last long, though. My mother's job ended and we changed schools before the first semester concluded.

"It was the eighth grade. My mom sent my sister and me to California to live with my single uncle. Uncle David was, and still is, a great role model and friend. Back then, he had no idea what to do with two girls aged 11 and 12 years old. We lived in a small apartment and he drove a yellow Volkswagen Beetle. That was one of the best years of my life."

"He had rules and we were good kids. But, oh! The mischief we got into. He allowed us to be kids and do things we had never done before. Every

Saturday, he would drop us off at the horse arena where we learned to ride horses. Riding horses was great! He also took us camping – I hated that. Being outside was awful. On Sundays, another uncle and his wife would pick us up for church. Sometimes they would keep us overnight and give Uncle David a break – they were good to us also; we loved being part of their families. Life was great again. We loved Uncle David and tried to stay out of trouble so he would let us stay another year. Unfortunately, at the end of the year, we went back home to Connecticut."

"It wasn't that I didn't love my mother and brother; I missed them terribly. I was always glad to go home but I just never knew what each day would bring. As an adult, I realize, I like stability and consistency. I don't like moving – I am a creature of habit, a homebody. I do not like change."

"I began the 9th grade in Bridgeport, Connecticut, with my new best friend, Joanie. We met when I returned to Connecticut. She was just as skinny as I was; so together we could endure the abuse the other kids directed at us because we were so skinny. It wasn't so bad because we had each other. We would just laugh and talk about them (when they couldn't hear us, of course). She was fun. She was Jehovah's Witness and I was Christian (Pentecostal). We were okay with that, but the adults in our lives were not. It created problems, but that's another story!"

"That year at high school there were lots fights. Race riots, and fights between the blacks and the whites. The Puerto Ricans stayed with the blacks and the Jewish kids would take the winner's side. It was a very tough year to be a skinny black girl in high school. Joanie and I would skip school if we thought there was going to be a fight. We were not fighters. Besides, when there was a big riot, the school would lock the students in the building, and the kids on the outside would try to tear down the building. I didn't think it was safe on the outside or the inside. I could hear my father on the outside, talking through the bullhorn trying to calm the black kids down. They always called him to talk to the black kids when there was a riot.

"During the summer before 10th grade, my mother decided to move to California. I thought I had died and gone to heaven for sure! I was glad to move closer to Uncle David and other family members. I thought life would be different. Unfortunately, my mother married that summer in Connecticut and off we all drove together to California. We ended up in San Jose and moved into a very nice home. My mother's husband worked and she stayed home. My mother cared for a foster child (Brian); he was such an amazing little kid. Her husband had a daughter who came to live with us. She did not like my sister and me, and we didn't like her. She was older and was miserable living with us.

"My brother, after a short stay in California, ended up going back to Connecticut to finish his senior year in high school. There was no family there, so he stayed with friends. My sister and I really missed him that year. As for the new husband, well, it turned out he was not a nice guy. Their marriage didn't last long. After they split up, Mother, Sister, and I moved into a very nice apartment in Sunnyvale, California. And that, of course, meant another change in schools, but I liked that school and made a lot of friends pretty easily. Unfortunately, we didn't stay long, and in a few months we moved in with my aunt and her family in Sacramento. They lived in a beautiful home, and we could catch one bus to school. That lasted a couple of months, and we moved again into our own apartment. My mother worked two jobs, so we were on our own to get to school. We were pretty mature and loved going to school, so that was no problem.

"After about six months, we moved into another apartment that was close to her job and less expensive. It was a nice apartment. This time I was bussed to a school that had very few minorities and lots of cowboys. It was culture shock for me. The African American kids knew where they could walk, who to talk to, and pretty much stayed out of the way of the 'popular white kids.' I didn't understand that and felt I could go anywhere I wanted and participate in anything they offered. After a few trips to the office, the principal and I agreed that this was not the school for me. Besides, they reviewed my transcripts and said I did not have enough credits to graduate. I was sent to continuation school.

"I was so disappointed! I had always wanted to go to college but felt that since I was in continuation school that would never happen. College was out! For as long as I can remember, I wanted to be a teacher and adopt a whole bunch of kids. *Now*, I thought, *they will never let me adopt because I didn't go to college.*

"Boy, did God know what He was doing! It turned out to be a great school for me. I could work at my own pace and earn credits. They said if I worked really hard, I could graduate. If I could graduate, I could go to college!

"That was a tough year for us at home. My mom met a new guy and married. I did not want to move again, so I stayed in that apartment and she moved. I had a job, so I could handle most of the rent, but I knew it wouldn't last long. After a couple months, my brother came out and stayed with me. A friend of my brother's moved in also. The three of us decided to move into a less expensive place, and moved into a very low-income apartment. I was still in high school, but it was home, and we could afford it!

"After moving, I continued to attend the same continuation school. I had a teacher, Jim, who realized I was not living with an adult. He called my dad in Georgia. I was so angry with him! My dad came out and asked me to move back with him, but I knew his wife did not want me there. I was tired of being where I wasn't wanted. In the end, my father agreed that if I stayed in school and Jim kept in touch with him, that I was better off living on my own in an apartment. Thank you, Lord!

"I stayed, and soon graduated high school! Jim helped me to take tests and complete forms for college. During the second semester, he enrolled me in a class at the community college, where I got an A. I was so proud of myself! From there, my father helped me get admitted to Ottawa University (OU) in Ottawa, Kansas. My sister and stepsister also attended the college, and we planned to move into an apartment and go to college together. They would have both been sophomores and I would be the freshman. I was elated.

"I spent the summer prior to attending OU in Atlanta, Georgia, with my dad and his family. I worked most of the time, so I wasn't around the house much. I saved enough money to buy a car. The problem was, I went out to buy the car by myself and some guys 'ripped me off.' I ended up with no money and no car to show for it. I was still determined to go to college, with or without a car. Well, I made it. Barely! But I made it to college.

"When we arrived at the college, it turned out my sister was unable to stay as she had not passed a class she needed, and my stepsister decided to spend that year in Kansas City. So, there I was: all alone and with no car. That was a sad day. But, I was determined to stay there, go to class, get a job, and graduate. I didn't need friends. Well…I wanted friends, but I just didn't have any. I prayed and asked the Lord to help me find a job so I could afford to stay there. I qualified for some grants and borrowed as much money as I could. I was eligible for a lot of grants and loans, but not enough to pay for everything. I decided I should get off the meal plan and save money, so I did. That meant I had to buy and cook food, but there was a rule that prohibited cooking in the dorm. No problem! I was able to get a job in the snack bar, which included one meal on each shift. Okay, Praise God! Later, I also found a job at a home for disabled adults and one meal was included with each shift—great! I bought some peanut butter and jelly, and some cereal, which I ate dry (I didn't drink milk anyway) and I was good. I made it through the first semester. Most students wondered why I never came to the cafeteria, but after a while they figured it out.

"I also prayed for a friend, just one friend, who would be a true friend. There was a girl across the hall that was nothing like me. The other girls in the dorm talked about how she had a baby at home. They wanted to stay away from her. I thought, *Wow, she might be a bit more mature than these other silly girls!* She and I hit it off from the beginning, and Linda and I are still friends today.

"I also met Alfred at Ottawa, but that is a whole different story.

"Lord, growing up with all the twists and turns was not easy. But, I thank you for every opportunity because all those experiences made me who I am today. I am so sensitive to people who are not wealthy because I know how it feels to do without. I understand how poor and wealthy people can get caught up in their selfish, 'pity-party' ways, and take their eyes off of You. You blessed me to live with both of them; please help them to keep their eyes focused on You.

"I know what it is to be a child and feel lonely, isolated, wanting an adult to depend on. Help me, Lord, to recognize those children as I live every day. Help me to be the adult that is loving and caring. Help me, Oh Lord, to be a good listener.

"Thank you! You were always there for me and you always provided me with an adult when I needed one. Thank you for my mother, and all that she did for her kids. When her life was shattered she didn't give up—she kept fighting. She made so many sacrifices and I'm sure I didn't always act appreciative. Thank you for her hard work. Thank you for all the adults You brought into my life; each one provided what I needed at that time. I even thank you, Lord, for Sister Magdala.

"Some people have wonderful childhoods, and others have childhoods that make them wonder if there is a God. Well, I pray that no matter what the childhood is like, that each one would look back and know that You, Oh Lord, were there every step of the way and kept them alive. I know that You kept me alive, You fed me, clothed me, and loved me. Thank you! In Jesus' name, Amen."

2

Can You Drive in the Snow?

In the beginning, she and I were committed to walking on opposite sides of the same road. She introduced herself by insulting me: "… Hey, are you the freshman named Yoyo?" There was a horrible sitcom that was entitled *Holmes and Yoyo*, which "starred" two nondescript characters whose only purpose was to insult the intelligence of every viewer. I retorted back at her question, "My momma did not name me Yoyo!" She was unimpressed and, as she left, continued mocking me with some of her upperclassmen friends. It was hard enough being planted in some far-off college in the middle of Ottawa, Kansas. She had the audacity to insult my name! It was the summer of 1977, and I never spoke to her again until the winter of 1980. Oh, I saw her on campus—OU was a small college—but seeing someone was one thing, acknowledging that we coexisted on the same planet was completely different. I was very prideful during that time, and she was stubbornly independent.

It was during a trip to Kansas City on an evening in December of 1979 that our lives became entangled permanently. Unbeknownst to one another, we had joined the same college gospel choir. I was a horribly average singer; she was only slightly better. We sang that night to a half-empty and halfhearted group of parishioners. The only thing more off-key than I was the kids asleep and snoring in their mommas' laps. We exited the church only to discover a fine layer of ice on the ground and on the windows of our vehicles. Sleet! It made driving the fifty miles back to OU a recipe for disaster. The first car skidded out of the drive onto the street as an inexperienced, overzealous college student pressed the accelerator.

"Is there anybody who is okay with driving in the snow?" she asked.

"It is sleet, not snow," I informed her. "It is like driving on ice…just steer and refrain from accelerating. The car will drive itself!"

"Refrain from what?"

She had a way of being sarcastic that made my bones ache.

"Where are you from?"

"Denver, Colorado."

"Will you drive my car?"

I paused. I wanted to ask her if she was going to be in the car with me, but understood that probably was not the right question to ask her. I told her "sure," and she asked, "What's your name?"

Surely she was kidding! I couldn't believe that she would allow a perfect stranger to drive her vehicle. "Al…Al Rowlett…and you?"

"Yvette Peters."

The fifty-plus-mile drive back was uneventful enough. Upon our arrival at OU, we dropped off the others and I drove myself to the back door of my dormitory. I felt a sense of accomplishment, and sounded almost cavalier when I asked her, "Do you want me to drive you home?" Yvette looked at me with those saucer-sized eyes and said, "No! I really don't know you that well. Anyway, how would you get back on campus?" Yvette lived off campus at the time.

"You don't think I am going to let you drive my car without me, do you?"

I was insulted. I had just spent one hour traveling with her and two other classmates and all I did was drive them back safely. I got out of the dark blue Mercury Zephyr and thought, *She is never going to make it.* The sleet was everywhere; even walking was treacherous. Yvette backed out of the parking stall and accelerated. I watched that Mercury Zephyr (or Squeaky, as she liked to call it) spin in a perfect

360, stopping almost exactly where she had started. She rolled the window down as I walked gingerly to the car and peered in.

"Are you sure you don't want me to drive?"

"I know how to drive, Al!" she sneered, rolling the window back up.

"Okay but remember when driving on sleet you have to let the car drive itself." I thought about asking her to call when she arrived at her apartment as she drove off. I envisioned her crashing her car, escaping unscathed but with her vehicle totaled.

The next few days passed uneventfully as the fall semester rapidly approached conclusion. I was debating whether I should buy a bus ticket home. It was my junior year (Yvette was a senior). I had not seen her or thought about her since the car ride from Kansas City. I was unaware that the Primary Person in our 28 years of marriage was putting in place a series of events that would forever change our lives. Yvette's father, Reverend Dr. James D. Peters, Jr., had recently been offered and accepted a Senior Pastor position at a church in, of all places, Denver, Colorado. I was raised in Denver; it was my home. Yvette had decided she was going to visit her father in Denver for Christmas. Some will assert that fate brought us together; others will say it was chance. I want to assure you it was the Holy Spirit; He was, and remained, the primary orchestrator of every major event in our lives.

When she remembered that I was from Denver, it made sense that she would ask me to drive her car 700 miles home from OU to Denver at the conclusion of finals. The only problem was that 700 miles was beyond her emotional tolerance of me. So, she asked an underclassman whom she deemed a friend of hers to ride with us. I drove the entire distance while she sat in the backseat, smoking cigarettes and talking to Chris (the underclassman). Only occasionally would she reference that my driving skills were pretty good. (Yes, I was intrigued by her insulting jabs.) When we arrived in Denver, a blanket of fresh snow that had fallen a few days prior had melted and had "*become a sheet of ice.*" That ice had been covered up during the day by a new layer of snow. Basically, the roads were super slick.

We dropped Chris off first. I lived a few minutes from Chris's home, so I insisted that Yvette come in and meet my family. I introduced her as Reverend Peters' daughter. She, of course, corrected me, stating, "Hello! I am Yvette!"

That made my father chuckle.

"I think she wants to be called Yvette!"

"Thank you," she responded.

I noticed a kind of human warmth when she acknowledged my father, something I did not think was possible.

My mother was less diplomatic: "Well, I am sure your father is anxious to see you."

This was code for "leave and come back another time, as long as you don't intend on marrying my son!" As Yvette walked out the door, my mother insisted that I follow her home. Yvette and I were stunned when she said it! I walked outside and approached her car. "I am going to follow you home."

"No!" she retorted.

She wasn't speaking to my father anymore; the warmth was replaced by the tone she used with me back at college. Inexplicably, I responded, "Yes I am." She looked flustered. Did I care about her? She was far too independent to need some momma's boy to care about her! I was shocked. *Why did I say that? What did I care if she drove off and crashed?* But I had said it, and I did it. As she drove off, I followed in my parents' Chevy Impala, all the while thinking, *Why am I doing this?* Predictably, I saw her car spin and slide—no, not a perfectly executed 360 this time, just one of those "you don't have control" reminders a driver gets when a car hits a patch of black ice. I got out of the car. She, of course, already had the window down and was ready to order me back to my car. I did not say a word. I just smiled, and she smiled also. That was the first time I thought, *Oh my goodness, do I like her?* The idea almost caused me to lose consciousness! I steadied myself against the trunk of her car and gingerly walked back to mine. I am sure she thought I was about to fall. *My Lord...I like her.* I continued mumbling it until we arrived at Monaco Boulevard and 26th Avenue;

she signaled and assured me she could make it home without my assistance. I acquiesced and returned home.

Christmas came and went; it was quite uneventful that year. Perhaps I was just distracted. One day, I got a message from one of my siblings that Yvette had called. She wanted to let me know where she could be reached in the event I needed to talk with her prior to returning to OU. I decided to seize the opportunity, and called her back to ask if she wanted to go to a party with some friends. She was very hesitant but agreed. I thought my charm and persistence won her over. Wrong! She was not won over. What I did not know at the time was that she had checked in to a Howard Johnson's hotel, and was staying there for the remainder of the break until after New Year's. When I picked her up from the hotel, I asked if everything was okay. She gave me the look a sympathetic owner is about to give a pet, that sort of superior-yet-pitying look prior to euthanizing it. I looked back at her, perplexed, wondering what I did wrong. "No!" Yvette was at times abrupt in her refusal to talk about a subject. "Okay."

I would get her back. I was double-dating, sort of. I had neglected to tell her I was escorting another longtime female friend. Yvette, my date, and my future groomsman (who also had two girls with him) went out to a party together. Yvette was surprised. She sat in the back of the car as we drove to the party, and she repeatedly asked my other date how long we had been together. I responded with great satisfaction, "We're just friends!" Something I repeatedly emphasized. "…We are just friends, Yvette." She never believed me, and subtlety was not her forte: she reiterated throughout the evening that we made a great couple.

After the party, I dropped my first date off and then I dropped Yvette off at her hotel. I invited myself in to her room, as I had an unquenchable curiosity as to why she was there instead of at her father's home. Yvette was direct. "You are either being nosey or caring. Which is it?" "You choose," I replied. I sighed at the notion of being cast out of the Howard Johnson's Hotel. Yvette looked at me and sized me up. She seemed to determine that I was harmless enough and that all I really wanted to be was a nice guy. I walked Yvette to her room and we ended up talking for about two hours. It seems Yvette and her stepmother got into an awful argument when she arrived on the first night. It was decided then that she should check in to a hotel. She didn't mind as she had room service and uninterrupted visits by her father. I was appalled. I thought, *How horrible to spend Christmas and New Year's in a hotel!* When I made my feelings known, she was insulted and wanted no part of my pity. I was quickly ushered out of her room. As I walked to my car, I knew she kind of liked me, and that I was starting to really like her.

Like all good things, the winter break finally ended and it was time for us to return to OU. Yvette and I met at my house (with a brief stop at my aunt's to get her to cash a Christmas check). Our other passenger, Chris, had decided to drop out of college. He was not going back, so we were going to be alone in the car together for 700 miles. I gulped at the prospect. His decision to drop out of college was the topic of conversation for the first 6–7 minutes, after which we quickly realized that there were hundreds of miles to go, and we would still have to talk to each other. It was approximately 5 p.m. in Denver; OU was 12 hours away, and we both had classes the next morning. Twelve hours later, we arrived at OU unscathed. I was surprised at how alert I was, almost euphoric. What was initially awkward and difficult became a fascinating 12-hour discussion about family, future, and our faith in Christ Jesus. We dared to talk about our fears, hypocrisy of the faith involving religious denominations, and the mantra about the Holy Spirit. We enjoyed each other's company but refused to acknowledge it when we arrived at OU.

3

Going a Long Way

There comes a point in almost every friendship when you have to decide. We reached that point in the spring of 1980. We thought we wanted to go to Denver for spring break, and since she had a car and wanted to visit her dad in Denver, I bummed a ride. The prospect of spending spring break at OU was about as appealing as eating cafeteria food. We agreed on a departure time and began what was, at first, a slow and arduous drive to Denver, as we were both exhausted from midterms. A recent snowstorm had dumped several inches of snow on the interstate. As we began talking about the long drive ahead and various other things, Yvette said, "I don't really want to go to Denver."

I was stunned and silent, because neither did I. Then she added, "I just came because I thought you wanted to go to Denver."

That was code seldom used by Yvette, and I interpreted it as, *maybe she likes me.* I laughed and said, "I just wanted to be with you, too! That is why I decided to go to Denver." We had traveled approximately 300 miles to reach this figurative crossroads: we could keep going to Denver, or we could turn around and spend the next three days on campus getting to know one another. We agreed and, in the middle of Interstate 70, slowed, did an illegal U-turn, and headed back to OU. I was giddy. Yvette was laughing hysterically.

Then she asked me the question. "So, Alfred Rowlett, what does this mean?"

A long pause followed. "I think it means we like each other." There...I had said it. I sounded like a soprano that just had a tonsillectomy.

"Well! Is that what it means?" Yvette asked in an almost mocking manner. I looked at her and she looked back at me; she killed me in any staring contest, but I just waited. She finally said, "Yes. I do like you, Al."

Wow, what a relief! Her ability to get me to go first was amazing. She was always so transparent, yet an independent fighter to the end. "Okay, I like you too." I looked at a highway sign; Lawrence, Kansas, was a few miles away, and we'd arrive at OU in less than an hour. Almost six hours had gone by, but it seemed like six minutes.

Spring break week was wonderful; I did not mind eating cafeteria food with Yvette. We would talk all night and never seemed to grow tired of each other's company. We almost forgot that over eighty percent of the student body was on break. Monday morning, the cold chill of reality was thrust upon us when her roommate told me that she thought we were crazy. "She is leaving, going to begin her life! Why would she want to get involved with you during your junior year? That's crazy! You two are different, very different; you're boring and she is exciting." On the other hand, it seemed like the more her friends said no, the more she defied them. "Al, who are you going to listen to," she snapped, "...me or them?" Yvette did not conform to any worldly standard. If the world said no, she would prove everyone wrong. The only opinions that mattered were God's, hers, and now, occasionally, mine.

How we made it to her graduation date remains vague and unclear. Among finals, arguments, interfering friends, and concerns about our families, I don't remember much about it at all. I am not sure we ever announced to anyone other than her roommate that we were officially dating, but they knew. People would look at us and say, "You two are crazy!" At an end-of-the-year picnic, I thought every student at the small college was staring at us. We were like animals on display. People would approach us separately and ask, "Are you crazy? She is graduating! What are you going to do?"

Her graduation finally arrived. I knew she was very committed to including me in family gatherings and introducing me to everyone; however, I was a bit reluctant. I felt like a giant sea turtle stranded on a beach: out of my element. I just was not ready for the onslaught. I decided after my first meeting that I would only occasionally come out of my resident director's dorm room. When I did come out, I was introduced to the whole family: her father, James Daniel Peters, Jr., referred to lovingly as "Deddy" (the 'a' in Daddy was pronounced with an 'e' sound); mother, Ida Dee Garrett (called "Mother-dear" or "Mother" by many and later "Nana"); brother, James Daniel Peter III, "James III" (later "Uncle Jimmy"); and sister, Pamela Peters (later "Aunt Pommie"). Yvette would regularly bring family members over to meet the new boyfriend. Everyone was cordial, except James III; he threatened to shoot me for getting too close to his sister. "Oh! Are you one of the people I need to shoot?" he bellowed at me. "My sister is too good for you!" No matter—soon graduation weekend would be over and I could begin preparing for the summer session and my senior year. Or so I thought. The night before graduation, I came out of the room, and my turtle shell, to eat. I am not suggesting that I was a coward! It was just my apprehension about meeting Yvette's family. After gulping down my dinner in approximately three minutes in the OU cafeteria, I remember returning to my dorm and noticing figures in front of the door to my room. It was Yvette, she was with her family, and they insisted that I join them for dinner. "Sure!" I squealed like a rat that had just been caught by the trap. "I would be glad to join you!" Yvette gave me the look she used to give the children when they were caught lying. She just knew how to read me better than I ever could read her. She could hide or reveal her displeasure behind her eyelids and only the Holy Spirit knew what she was really thinking.

The dinner took three days to complete with Mother Dear vividly reliving Yvette's exploits as a child and saying how she never thought that little girl would be the first to finish college.

"Yvette was the most aggravating child in the world sometimes. She would say, '...Oh Mother, do we really need to do this?' She would convince Pam and Jimmy to follow her; they would get into all kinds of trouble! I remember the time they decided to build tents in the living room. They hammered the blankets and sheets into the wall with nails to keep them up. We had nail holes in the living-room wall! Or the time she was talking on the telephone, sitting on the floor, and kicking my 100-gallon fish tank with her foot. The tank somehow fell over and there went 100 gallons of water on my new carpet!"

The stories went on all throughout the meal. Afterwards, they deposited me back at the dorm, bid me good night, and drove off to return to their rooms. Prior to going to bed, my evening routine was interrupted by a knock on my door. It was Yvette. "Yvette, hey, how are you?" I asked, and started to give her a hug. She stopped me cold with what our daughter today insightfully refers to as "the wide-eyed look." She said, "I do not want you to ever avoid me. Okay? And do not believe all those stories. True, they happened, but not the way you heard them tonight." All right, I was a bit undone by the manner and tone. She was very angry. That night we talked for a long time about family, friends, and growing up. I listened...she talked and talked. I remember her candor and transparency being so refreshing. God was first in her life, and she did not care if the opinion of others contradicted her own as long as I understood the truth. She concluded, "God must have really been watching over me." After listening to her version of her life story, I had to agree.

Sometimes you find out the Lord has a sense of humor and that there is a lot you do not know. I was inexperienced and naïve. For example, when graduation was over and the campus was rapidly emptying, I was going to be the summer resident hall director, so I assumed I could stay on campus as long as I wanted. I did not know that everyone had to leave the campus for two weeks prior to summer session so they could clean and fumigate the dorms. They were going to be fumigating Price Hall (the dorm I was going to be staying in as the Summer Director), so I would have to leave campus for two weeks. I was unprepared, and could not afford to purchase a bus or plane ticket to Denver. Yvette insisted strongly that I travel in the car with her family to Denver. Her mother and cousin, Shelia, were going to Denver to assist Yvette with getting an apartment prior to returning to their home state of California. "Okay!" I said unenthusiastically and went to my apartment to gather my things.

I know what is written in the book of Daniel about the three Hebrews Shadrach, Meshach, and Abednego when Nebuchadnezzar, the Babylonian king, confronted them "…We do not need to defend ourselves before you in this matter. If we are thrown into the blazing furnace, the God we serve is able to save us from it, and He will rescue us from your hand, O king. But even if He does not, we want you to know, O king, that we will not serve your gods or worship the image of gold you have set up." Given the story, I know the fiery furnace was hot, but, in comparison to what I was about to do, maybe the fiery furnace was better. I wondered if the Holy Spirit was going to meet me in the car. I got in Mother Dear's black Chrysler Cordova like a cat that doesn't want to be stuffed in a cage and taken to the vet. They seemed poised as I got in the car. All I heard was the door of her mother's black Chrysler closing. *I'm doomed!* I thought. *They will probably drop me off in the middle of Kansas at a rest stop after they finish me off.* I longed for the blazing furnace. Yvette drove, initially. I thought this was going to work; with her mother and cousin in the backseat, I figured she would drive the entire trip. I was hiding the fact that I did not have a current valid driver's license. Given the euphoria of graduation, I figured it would take at least eight hours before she experienced any fatigue. Yvette drove for approximately one hour! After that she abruptly pulled over at a rest stop and said, "Okay, I'm tired…you drive."

I froze; I had to tell her. "I don't have a driver's license." I was whispering.

"You what? You don't have a what?"

Her mother pounced on me.

"What did he say, Yvette? I don't want him to drive my car if he can't drive."

"There is a problem with my license," I explained.

Shelia bellowed, "He does have one!"

Her mother demanded that Sheila be quiet.

"You don't have to possess a license to drive. All kinds of stupid folks got licenses and can't drive at all. Can you drive?"

"Yes!" Although my response inspired little confidence. Next thing I knew, I was behind the wheel and we were once again traveling on Interstate 70, heading to Denver. I could drive, and soon forgot that my license was expired. I was jolted back to reality when Yvette's mother said, "Hey, look, everybody pays their own tickets. So, you can keep driving 69 miles per hour, below the 70-mile-per-hour speed limit, or you can drive 85 like everybody else and if you get a ticket you will pay it."

I acquiesced, and sped up to 75 miles per hour. When we arrived in Denver safely, and without any speeding tickets, I hugged Yvette and walked up the steps to my parents' home, wondering when I would see her again.

That summer was filled with long sighs by us, during telephone conversations. We also communicated in letters—some of the sappiest love letters ever written. "The sun is shining arrows" was her catch-phrase. I had returned to OU; she had gotten a job as a reading teacher. We were in love. My senior year at OU began with me avoiding the M-word, so Yvette asked me, "So, when are you going to ask me to marry you?"

4

Family Time

They say that when you love someone, you will do anything for them. Well, I would say that defying my father ranks up there for me...or should I say attempting to defy my father? It was November of my senior year in college and we wanted desperately to be married. Yvette had driven from Denver to visit me for the Thanksgiving break. She was staying in a friend's apartment. One evening I decided to call my father and mention the 'M' word. I remember that conversation all too well:

"Hello, Dad! How are you?"

"Fine, who is this?"

"It's your son, Alfred!"

"I have a son named Alfred? Okay, what can I do for you?"

"Well! Yvette and I want to get married, this month!"

I don't know how long my father actually held his breath for, but I am confident he stopped inhaling for some time. All I heard were gasps on the telephone. He was shocked and disappointed in me. In just a few months, I would be going across the stage as the family's first college graduate. He was clearly considering a proper response to what he considered an improper proposition. I wondered how he was going to say he was opposed to the idea.

Finally he said, "What? Where are you going to live? In the barracks?"

"No, I live in an apartment on campus. She will live with me here."

"In the barracks!"

He was in no mood to negotiate. He equated living in a dormitory to living in army barracks. It was unsuitable for any woman, let alone his future daughter-in-law. I missed the point totally; I interpreted his response as a "NO" or vote of disapproval of our union, not as a disapproval of our timing. His assertion was that his son was not thinking logically. What he was really saying was "get married after you graduate and don't force your wife to live in the barracks with you!" I was frustrated; Yvette was disappointed. She knew I could not openly defy my father.

The remainder of the weekend seemed to be going somewhat uneventfully. Thanksgiving came, and I had prepared a small meal for us. Yvette showed up early as we both wanted to watch the Cowboy's game and then have dinner. The telephone rang, and Yvette answered. I noticed that she almost recoiled when she said hello. Then she turned to me with an astonished look on her face, handed me the telephone, and said softly, "I think it is your mother."

I took the telephone, believing that her eldest son could easily dissuade any animosity or disappointment that may have been created as a result of my telephone conversation with Dad. Oh, how I was mistaken!

"Hello, Mom!" I was interrupted by a person who was clearly angry and crying. "Alfred, this is your mother. You remember me? The person who carried you around and fed you for nine months? Oh! You may not remember that, but I do. I want you to remember that on holidays and birthdays that you are able to celebrate them today because of what your momma did for you then. Make sure you remember that; I hope you have a Happy Thanksgiving!"

There was a deafening silence in the room. I wanted to scream, but I could not. It was the first time in four years that I felt alienated from my family. Yvette stared at me.

"Babe, are you okay?"

"What did you say?" I responded.

"I asked if you were okay."

"No! What did you call me?"

"Babe!"

She gave me a hug and we sat down. We ate and talked for twenty-four hours without interruption. After that, I was forever cemented in her life as "Babe." Yvette drove back to Denver and began planning the Big Wedding. She and I (more she than I) decided to get married at New Hope Church in Denver, Colorado, on May 30, 1981. My parents were sort of excited, especially since we had decided to wait until after graduation. Every conversation that we had following that Thanksgiving Day was regarding the wedding. It was during one evening in December, after I had grown tired of studying and had gone to bed, that I was awakened by a telephone call.

"Babe, this is Yvette. I have bad news…your parents' house caught on fire."

"What did you say?"

"Their house caught on fire. Dad and Mom are okay. Mom is very upset!"

As a result of this disaster, the relationship between Yvette and my mother began to develop. The fire was a source of sadness, grief, and loss for years. Yvette was on the scene trying to comfort and console Mom. I was in Kansas wanting desperately to get home to help. There were no cellular telephones, only what we describe today as "rotary dinosaurs." Information was very limited. I remember talking to my father and all he could say was, "…I don't know, Al!"

My mother conveyed the loss in every uttered word.

"We lost everything…pictures…the Bible…everything. It's awful!"

After finals, I caught the bus from Ottawa to Denver. Yvette picked me up from the bus station. "I want you to understand a couple things, Babe; Mom is very upset about the losses. You guys lost everything in the fire. The inside of the house was completely destroyed and the basement was heavily damaged by smoke from upstairs. Mom lost her pictures and her Bible." I understood the magnitude of the loss when she said that. The large white Bible that sat on the coffee table every day of my life, as long as I could remember, the one that had everyone's information, their histories, was gone. My family was temporarily staying with my mom's older sister, Aunt Helen. We arrived at my aunt's home; she was gracious and excited to see me. I knew this was a difficult transition for all of them, I just did not understand how difficult. I realized during the two weeks of that winter vacation that the umbilical tie between my parents and me was being cut. I was being re-grafted to another person. I lived with them during the two-week period, not fully comprehending that it would be the last time that I would reside with them for more than fourteen days. Yvette understood, and began to speak to me about our future together.

During winter break we agreed to visit her mother in California in the spring. While there, we were going to go shopping for an engagement ring. I was really going to marry her; there was no turning back. I was scared to death, but she was confident for both of us. Our spring break visit with Mother Dear was an amazing experience. Engagement-ring shopping with my future mother-in-law was hilarious. Mother Dear, Yvette, and I purchased the engagement ring at Devon's Jewelry Store in Sacramento, CA. Yvette was reluctant to buy anything too flashy as she did not want it to appear pretentious. For my part, I wanted the cheapest thing in the case. We shopped for hours; I agonized over every step. Mother Dear ignored my moaning as a senseless distraction. I tried to get Yvette's attention as she looked through the glass at the rings.

"What do you think, Babe? Babe got money?" she chuckled. "Mother Dear is going to pay the down payment on the ring, okay?"

That meant I was on my own regarding the monthly engagement ring payments. Suddenly and loudly, Mother Dear exploded, "Yvette, you are not going to mess around and get something gaudy like some of the people in this store."

Have you ever been in a mall and suddenly everything stops moving? I have. Everyone in the Devon's Jewelry Store stopped moving. I was standing at the entrance. Yvette came rushing out looking flushed, something that only happened with the frequency of a lunar eclipse.

She was never flustered. I asked, "What happened?" They both scurried past me like mice that had just escaped an alley cat. I wondered what had happened. As I gazed into the jewelry store, everyone seemed to be peering at me like I was about to lose a gunfight. I turned, only to hear Mother Dear say, "If he is stupid enough to stand there, too bad for him!"

I was sure there was more to the story as Yvette came back to quickly retrieve me. I was told later that Mother Dear had actually suggested a particular group of people were gaudy, only to observe that they were the patrons in that particular jewelry store. No surprise, we settled on the much less conspicuous Devon's in a different mall and purchased Yvette's ring.

The race to May 30, 1981 started the day I returned to college. Ours was going to be the wedding for the ages. I was content to be a bystander with one, maybe two, lines to repeat in the process. "I do—in sickness and in health until death do us part!" In retrospect, I did not realize the prophetic nature of those words and their eternal consequences. However, in every race there are those moments when something happens to test the stamina and internal fortitude of some of the participants. Yvette was about to face her greatest test. A few days before my family was at the point of reoccupying the house on Dahlia Street, Yvette was invited over for a "brief chat." My mother and my aunts were all waiting for her in the living room. She described the exchange as an attempt to derail the wedding, or certainly the timing of the wedding.

"Oh! They were waiting for me and I was by myself. They wanted to know if I was pregnant, and what the big hurry was to get married if I wasn't? They told me that you were perfect! Come on—Babe... perfect? Nobody is perfect, except Jesus. Lord Jesus! When I told them that I did not think you were perfect, your mom wanted to kill me. When I finally was able to leave, Deddy was waiting for me at his apartment with the same questions."

I tried to listen without saying anything. Yvette was furious. She wanted to leave Colorado and move back to Kansas.

"Babe, do you want to get married?"

"Sure!" I said meekly. There was a long pause, an awkward silence; she was saddened and unhappy at the prospect of marrying someone who sounded as uncommitted and dispassionate as I did.

She told me, "I will talk to you later." What followed was something I would never hear again in all my years of marriage to Yvette: dial tone. Two days later she called, but made no reference to the forty-eight-hour standoff. Yvette acted like it did not matter; she was not compelled to discuss it and neither was I.

5

Hello, I Am the Holy Ghost

The baptism of the Holy Spirit is often referred to as being like fire caught up in the bones of a believer. There is no doubt I was apprehensive, and only mildly curious, about what it meant to receive the baptism. In the spring of 1981, there was a crusade being waged by one student in particular who had the audacity (at least, that is what I considered it at the time) to pray for students so they could receive the baptism. His name was William. His claim was legitimized by an outward manifestation by the students for whom he prayed: "*Speaking in Unknown Tongues.*" Many students, including William, were going around speaking and praying in other tongues. My religion was important to me. I had been a Baptist all my life. Consequently, I had decided I was not going to have any part in this crusade taking place at OU. One day, while sitting in the cafeteria William asked me, "Hey, Al, have you received the Baptism?" "No!" I barked defiantly. "It does not mean you are saved. I don't speak in other tongues and I am saved." Silence. Everyone at the table was looking at me.

William was more interested in the theological reasons for my rebuttal. It did not bother him that I barked; he just attributed it to religious doctrine, or so I thought. He never really told me what he taught. He just seemed curious. I telephoned Yvette later that evening and told her what happened. She was surprised at my revelation and righteous indignation. "Babe, I received the Baptism and I speak in tongues." I was stunned. This epitomized our relationship; she was always surprising me! That night Yvette encouraged me to explore the depth and breadth of the Holy Spirit. I was comfortable with my religious, narrowly defined understanding of Him. I even referred to the Holy Spirit consciously as "It" (Holy Spirit, please forgive my ignorance). He was not a counselor or friend; I saw Him as an unknown celestial being from a distant planet. I was comfortable with the relationship until Yvette's revelation; after that, I needed to know more. "When and how did you receive the baptism?" I listened intently. I was perplexed! I thought I'd known everything about her; I felt like I knew nothing at all after our conversation. Religiously, I was the one in control, whereas she was comfortable moving outside of the norm and letting Him take control. I walked according to a rigid precast doctrine; she listened and solicited numerous evangelists and preachers for perspective and had received the baptism. There was no doubt: I could not marry her without getting "It" myself. I decided one Saturday evening that I was going to receive the baptism, or else! I waited until dark, because I knew God only showed up in a mysterious way and that meant "It" wanted darkness. I knelt down adjacent to the couch in the front room of my tiny dorm-style apartment and waited. I began to pray. I felt nothing special but persisted in praying. After several hours of frustration and, yes, even tears, I went to bed. Maybe "It" was busy, or I was not ready.

The following week I began to understand the nature of Yvette's relationship with the Lord. Some of her gifts lay dormant and unused until she met me. Or, as she said, "I need my gifts to be activated if I am going to survive being married to you." She was always blunt and honest, and in this case I was inclined to agree. Still, how was she able to receive "It"? The week following my Saturday night of prayer was a disaster. I was frustrated. I spent many hours kneeling in front of the couch waiting for the special moment when I would break the silence in the room with a chorus of tongues. I thought, *My tongues will surely be in a Hebrew dialect.* Still nothing, and I grew more frustrated and skeptical with each passing day. The only things that appeared were marks on my knees from all that praying. During one of my telephone calls with Yvette, she finally said what I knew we were both thinking: "So why don't you ask him to pray for you?"

"Who are you talking about?" I asked, because I was insulted. The suggestion nauseated me; my pride was like an avalanche that came cascading down upon that telephone. What was I supposed to say? "Why don't you pray for me, since it is obvious I am not good enough?" I recoiled at the notion of begging William to pray for me. I was religious. *Too religious?* I wondered. She was quiet; I waited for her to say she needed to get off the telephone. She remained quiet, and I finally gave in, as the silence was deafening. "Okay," I said, "I will talk with him tomorrow."

That night my prayers were like clanging symbols, as I had become a Pharisee. Not just metaphorically speaking, but literally: I was on the main floor of the dormitory and my spiritual nemesis (William) lived in the basement. I started praying well before midnight, and I stopped at about one o'clock in the morning. After some not-so-subtle and completely ineffective begging for God to bless me, I relented. It was like He was telling me, "You said you don't need the gift!" I walked downstairs, fully expecting to knock on my nemesis's door, awaken him, and ask for prayer that would, of course, result in nothing. I thought for a moment, *What if he was breaking a rule?* Then I could dump a reservoir full of hypocrisy on him. To my dismay, I could clearly see from the top of the flight of stairs that he was not only awake (because his light was shining underneath the door of his room), but he didn't appear to be breaking any rules. He was listening to gospel music and was playing it loudly. I knocked on the door like a pimply-faced teenager, looking for a reason to hang up the telephone before the girl he had a crush on could answer. The music ceased, and in an instant the door opened.

There is an awkward moment that occurs for a young man the first time he truly understands what his mother means when she proclaims to the entire family that "...it was hard to wean him off breast milk." The visualization can cause blindness, and the raucous laughter following can result in hearing loss. I was caught in the most awkward of moments, given I had knocked only once on his door. He opened the door and I spoke: "Hey man, I was wondering if you could pray for me so I could receive 'It'…you know, the baptism?"

He responded like the parent of the wayward child that had just come back home. "Sure, man!"

The next twelve seconds will be forever sealed in my heart and mind; it seemed to take a day and lasted no longer than twelve seconds. He prayed one, two, maybe three audible words that were followed by simple instructions. "Al, you pray, just not in English."

William had some oil that he kept in a very small glass container; he placed it delicately on his fingertips and touched my head. He might have said *"Dear God"*; however, before he could utter another word, a torrent of praise came rushing out of my mouth. It was like a gale-force windstorm of words of praise. None of the words spoken were in English and these words were coming out of my mouth! I wanted to take off my head so I could see me. *What was coming out of my mouth?* After a few seconds, I looked at William and said, "… Thank you very much." I politely turned and headed back to my dorm apartment.

I wonder at what point God says, *"I got you!"* Upon entering the door I felt the overwhelming urge to thank the creator of the universe for saving my life and imparting the gift upon his anally retentive servant. I prayed, thanking God for not killing me with a bolt of lightning. By then, it was almost two o'clock in the morning. I wanted to telephone Yvette and tell her; she would want to be the first to know. I think I realized that I loved her at that point, as I wanted to tell her before anyone else. But it would have to wait until tomorrow. She was living with her father, and he might not appreciate a 2:00 a.m. telephone call. I called home, and remarkably both of my parents answered the telephone simultaneously. I said, "Mom and Dad…I can speak in tongues!" I could practically hear my dad thinking, *Did God tell you to call us at 2:00 a.m. to tell us?* Dad was always practical. My mother said, "Son, now you know you are saved!"

The next morning I telephoned Yvette before she went to work. In her usual fashion, she got right to the heart of the matter when I told her that I received the baptism of the Holy Spirit.

"It is about time! What took you so long? I have to go to work, but we will talk later."

6

How the Family Grew

Yvette would often describe the family in ways that caused us all to stare at her, as she always depicted us as a *"half-full glass."* For her, it was all about the journey:

"What an amazing journey my kids and I have been on! They have no idea the joy they bring to me. When Alfred and I were married, we had our first child in that same year, a girl, LaTyia Annette Vernease. She was perfect. Eighteen months later, we had another little girl, Kimberly Twan-Raeone. You guessed it: another perfect child. About 3 years later, we decided to begin the process of adoption. What we didn't know (but I'm sure God knew) is that we would end up with 2 little boys just 8 weeks later: Kirkland Mario, who was almost 3 years old, and Tyler Maurice, who was 12 months younger than his brother.

"So, here we were with four little children, ages 2-4 years old. The girls were 18 months apart, Kimberly and Kirkland were three months apart, and Tyler was twelve months younger than Kirkland. God has a sense of humor for sure. We could hardly afford the two kids we had; we didn't even have a car large enough to fit everyone. We had some kind of faith! I don't think we even knew what we were getting into.

"Then one day a child named Trey Harold, who was four years old, came for a visit. He stayed with us for a couple months during the summer; his grandmother decided that she wanted him to return to Denver prior to kindergarten. I felt so torn about him going back. I remember praying and asking the Lord what He wanted. I believe the Lord spoke to me then and let me know it was okay to send him there; He also let me know that Trey would be back and we would be raising him. I sent him back, and waited for the Lord to reveal His plan for Trey.

"Life went on. Three years later, we would get the call from his grandmother asking us to raise him. This time, we insisted on legal guardianship papers and, within a few weeks, I was on a plane going to Denver to get Trey. I had just been diagnosed with sarcoidosis, and it would have been easy to say 'No!' But the Lord had already told me the call would come one day, so I trusted Him and went to Denver. I must admit, I thought, *Lord, are You sure about this?* I had my doubts about my health, but there was no hesitation about Trey.

"So, now there were five kids: 7, 11, 12, 13, and 14 years old. Life was busy! We split our time between church, dancing, and soccer. Everyone was involved in something in addition to school, homework, and daily chores. My health was good, but I knew I had this disease with no cure. I had to avoid colds, the flu, and kids, according to my doctors. Yeah, right!

"Well, as God would have it, Hannah Yvette came into our lives. She was a year old when I brought her home. We had established a relationship with her from birth, as my mother was her foster mother. God opened a door for us to adopt Hannah one year later: the county was prepared to remove Hannah from my mother's care and place her in a foster home. I went to the meeting and informed the county I had a mentor relationship with the child; they had to consider me as a prospective adoptive parent. Now all God had to do was to convince Babe that she was going to be a Rowlett forever. I was 44 years old, had a terminal illness, and Trey was in high school. *Why would we be starting this process all over again? God, are you sure?* Well, it took some convincing, but two years later we were signing the adoption papers. No one could have told me how much we would all love her, and how much joy she would bring to the Rowlett household. *Here we go again,* I thought. *God has given us another perfect child.*

"*Are we done yet, Lord?* Well, he gave us some respite until June of 2009. Yes, I had been through a year of cancer and had a year to recuperate when the call came. Culese, Trey's biological brother, would be coming to live with us. *Wow, Lord, are You sure? My health has been getting worse and we have been talking about me retiring or cutting back on work. He will be a senior in high school, and it's not like he and Trey will be living with one another. Trey is on the East Coast, in college. Really, God? Now?*

"I thought back and remembered when Trey came, and I was asking all of the same questions. I also remembered when Hannah came and I had so many doubts. God showed us it was the right thing at the right time. I didn't fight too much this time. As a matter of fact, after the call came, it was only one week later that we were picking him up from the airport.

"What was I thinking about with Culese? His biological mother had died a few years ago, and I wondered, *If the Lord calls me home soon, how would that affect him?* Yes, I thought about that for a minute, then I smiled at God and said, "That would be Your issue, God, not mine." That issue was more than I could bear to think of, but it's not too big for God.

"So, if you're counting, that makes seven kids. Yes, seven is a biblical number, but I've learned that God can do whatever he wants to do with my life and I trust Him. I learned over the years just how much I can trust Him. What does the future hold? I don't know, but God knows.

"Lord God,

We have no idea what the future holds, but as long as we know that You are in charge, we can sleep at night and be at peace. Thank You for blessing me with such a wonderful family, even though I don't deserve it. Each day, you teach me that I have more to pour into others' lives. Thank you for all the lessons in life that have shaped me to be the person that I am.

"I cannot thank you enough for my children. Yes, they cause me lots of heartache with some of their choices, but You, Lord, have taught me and each day teach me how to love them through their trials and tribulations.

"I pray, Lord, that I will live to see each of them serving You in the ways that would be pleasing to You. I pray that You will continue to teach each one to be the man or woman that You desire for them to be.

"Thank you for their husbands and wives. Oh, they have so much life to experience! I pray that they will lean on You for everything; that they will be good Christian spouses, fathers, mothers, and coworkers. Let my daughters and daughters-in-law be good, virtuous women and let my sons and sons-in-law be mighty men of God.

"I pray for my grandchildren, that You will teach me, Lord, how to be a good 'granny' to them. If they experience me with an oxygen tube attached to my nose, Lord, I pray that they see beyond that and see me as You would have them see me.

"Lord, I ask that you allow me to spend many years with them and pour into their lives. The relationship between a child and his/her grandmother is so important. I remember my granny, and how much she poured into my life. Even though we didn't live in the same state, I remember the times we spent together and the stories she would tell me. Her love for me has extended past her time on this earth. Lord, you know the impact she had on my life and I thank You for the time we had together. Lord, I thank you for the relationship my dad had with his mother, and how much that has influenced my life. Grandmother loved her son; as she used to say, 'Mary could not have been more proud of Jesus than I am of James.' Wow, what a statement, Lord! I don't know about Mary and Jesus, or if Mary ever thought about such a thing, but that statement is an example of their love.

"Lord, teach my children to be good parents. Thank you for my children, their spouses, and my grandchildren. Thank you for the love we have for one another. Lord, I ask You to allow others to experience true love for their children no matter how they act; You loved us steeping in sin, so help us to love others that may be steeping in sin now. You are our hope. Thank you. In Jesus' Name, Amen."

7

Women United

"Over 18 years ago, some friends named Lola and Michael were expecting their second child. Renita, Angela, and I got together and decided to give her a baby shower. We didn't want this to be just any ordinary baby shower, so we decided to do the usual games and stuff, but to also have a Bible study as part of the shower.

"The shower turned out to be a success. She received some really nice gifts, and the four of us decided that bringing women together to study the Word of God was encouraging. We continued that Bible study once a week, and it is fondly and lovingly known as the 'Thursday Night Bible Study.' Over the past 18 years, we have met on just about every night of the week, changing nights as our lives and needs changed. The four ladies, Angela, Lola, Renita, and myself, are the mainstays. It would not be an exaggeration to say that over a hundred women have attended the Bible study over the years. Many women and their families have been blessed by this Holy Spirit–directed ministry.

"We don't go to the same church, or even belong to the same denomination. We all love the Lord and have a desire to grow closer to Him. We all had young children when we started, and we wanted to raise them knowing and relying on the Word. We wanted to live our lives as examples, showing them what good Christian women could do if they trusted the Lord. Oh yes, we made many, many mistakes along the way, but I believe all our children know that we tried our best to be good examples and to raise them to love God.

"We have watched one another, our children, and, yes, even our husbands, grow up. We have cried together, laughed together, and gotten into all kinds of mischief together. We were always there for one another.

"Having close Christian women as friends has made me a better person, wife, mother, sister, coworker, and child of God. They will look me in the eye and tell me when I'm wrong and when I need to "…get over myself." They will cry with me when I hurt, but only for a little bit. For a few minutes one might cry with me, and the next one will say, 'Okay, pity party over, now what are you going to do?'

"They continuously point me to the Word and ask me if my actions, thoughts, or ideas are aligned with God's will for my life. They tell me when my kids are doing right or wrong, and ouch! Sometimes that really smarts! No matter how annoyed I get with them, I love them and appreciate them. They are my family and I thank the Lord for them daily.

"I love them so much, I cannot imagine going through life without them. My children would not have turned out the way they have if I didn't have these women to listen to me, be there when I needed to vent, and chastise me when it was warranted. I am safe sharing my fears with them, and they make me accountable to God when it is necessary.

"If you are a woman and don't have good Christian female friends, I suggest you pray and ask the Lord to send some to you. I remember early on in my marriage, I asked the Lord to send me a really good friend: a bosom buddy, like in *Anne of Green Gables*. I was serious, and the Lord knew that. He sent me not one, but three, and they have been a blessing in my life. I thank the Lord for that. I remember praying for a friend. I don't journal like I probably should, but I did this time. The Lord reminded me of the things I asked for, and when He provided me with friends I was always thankful. I love the Lord for doing that!

"When I was younger, friends were harder to come by. By the time

I graduated from high school, I had attended 18 schools over the years. It was a lot of moving around, and it felt like as soon as I made a friend I would leave them. Keeping friends was very tough; I would write letters, but it didn't take long before we would lose contact with one another. My brother and sister were my best friends. We were always there for each other, no matter how many times we moved. Still, I wanted friends and friendships that would sustain me through my lonely days.

"When I went to college, I felt pretty alone. I remember praying and asking the Lord for a female friend that would remain a friend even if we were living in different states, married with husbands, and starting families. God heard that prayer, and Linda Kay and I became friends for life. We are so different from one another, now and during college, but she was the perfect friend for me. We had rooms across the hall from one another as freshman, and became friends as a result of the close proximity. Even when I was forced to move into the dorm next door due to financial reasons, we remained close friends. I remember the day we finally moved into a house and then an apartment together. We lived together for the last two years of college. After college, she stayed in Kansas and I moved to California. Even in different states, we have remained friends. I don't talk to her every day, or even once a month, but when I call it's just like we talked the day before. We've been out of school for 28 years, but I can still call her and talk about anything. She is a true Christian friend."

"*Dear Lord,*

Thank You for one more day to appreciate the women You have brought into my life. Thank You for teaching me how to love them and how to encourage them, but more importantly, Lord, thank You for teaching them how to love me and provide the love I need on a daily basis.

"I love the Thursday Night Bible Study ladies and I love their husbands. They have given so much to me and my family—more than money, gifts, or other treasures. They have given their time, which has blessed me so much.

"Lord, I ask that if there is someone out there who does not understand what it is to have a real bosom buddy that You would bless them with one, and that they would know that person is a treasure. Thank You for friends that last a lifetime. In Jesus' Name, Amen."

8

Until Debt Do Us Part

Usually when a couple gets started they plan to do many things—children, housing, finances, and travel. We didn't have a plan for any of those things. We were in love and we loved God. After we were married in Denver, we decided that it would be best for us to hitch up the covered wagon and roll out west. So we borrowed Deddy's 1981 black Cadillac Sedan Deville. We rented a U-Haul, got into the car, and drove out west for California. We had decided to start our life away from the friendly confines of Denver and to move to Sacramento, California. We agreed that it would be best, especially if we wanted to do things *our way*. We also wanted to give God the room to direct our lives; little did we know He was directing everything. So, we trusted in faith that it was the right decision. We had a grand wedding with many attendees. Most had come out to wish Reverend Peter's daughter the best. "Have a wonderful life together!" That was what most of our wedding guests told us. We had a U-Haul full of wedding gifts, no furniture, very little clothing, absolutely no appliances, and approximately $500. We were traveling to Sacramento to move in with Nana. Yvette cautioned me that our particular idiosyncrasies might not be easily digestible for Nana. Meaning, "Babe, Nana may not want to live with us, so don't be surprised. We might get there and she'll move out so we can stay in her place. She'll get her own place." Yvette was absolutely right. We arrived in Sacramento and, after only a few weeks, Nana was preparing to move out. We were living in the front unit of a four-plex. It was on Franklin Blvd; I will never forget—7524 Franklin Blvd. At times it was a peaceful oasis away from the business of looking for a job and dealing with other distractions. Other times it was right in the middle of the "…South Sac Hood." I remember one night there was a knock on our door. Yvette was pregnant; she looked out, and there was a bleeding young man at our door crying for help. Of course, she let him in. I came out and saw the gasping young man as he walked in our unit.

"Ma'am…ma'am, I need help. Could you please help me?"

Yvette looked at me and said, "Sure he'll help you."

She insisted that I set aside any refusal to help a fellow human being and act like a Christian. We put him in the backseat of our car and drove off to some part of North Sacramento. After approximately 30 minutes, we let him out in front of a house that I'm sure was a front for some kind of illegal drug operation, and drove back home. She looked at me and before I could get the words "*what were you thinking?*" out of my mouth, she said, "Don't say it! Just don't say it! We need to help people, Mr. Rowlett. That is why God put us on the planet, and that man needed some help. He is somebody's brother or maybe even somebody's father. Just don't say it."

I will always remember that day.

The following Sunday morning we were preparing to go to church. We had spent nearly every penny we had and were essentially broke. I was looking intensely at the paltry sum of money in my wallet that represented our entire net worth. Disgusted, I left the unit and walked outside. It was early in the morning as I stood outside by the car door. I looked down at the ground and there appeared to be something green sort of fluttering on the asphalt. I reached down and looked closely: it was a stack of dollar bills. I picked it up and walked back into the house and I showed it to Yvette. I said, "I wonder where this came from! Hmm, I wonder if our gang friend decided that those people were so nice who saved his life that he wanted to pay us." Who knows…it was what it was. We used that money to buy groceries, but our finances only got worse.

Since I couldn't get a job, and the opportunities for employment were not materializing, I decided that we needed to do something with those extra wedding gifts. Why did we need 13 salad bowls? And all those Crock-Pots? And the stoneware that didn't quite make a set? Off to Macy's we went. We returned many of our gifts for cash. At first, Yvette was understanding as we returned the salad bowls and Crock-Pots. However, it became "crystal-clear" to everybody at Macy's but me that this young couple didn't have any money, and that I was breaking my wife's heart. She stopped going to Macy's with me, and refused to go to JC Penney as I insisted on expanding the return parade. I think we got down to about six salad bowls and three Crock-Pots when I said, "…Maybe one day we'll need these Crock-Pots." She looked at me in a way that kind of reduces a man to miniscule size.

"You think maybe one day you will do something?"

That was code for, *You see I am pregnant. What is your excuse?* I was returning all of our wedding gifts and hadn't realized just how difficult that was for her. The gifts that people had individually selected for us, I was returning. She couldn't stand the idea. She was communicating that maybe one day I would become a man of God, but at that moment I was just a disappointing husband. In my mind I was doing the right thing—I was trying to stave off the inevitable: **welfare**.

Welfare. Instead of choosing to become a Godly servant, I chose food stamps. What does a young couple in their early twenties, recently graduated from college, want to do when they get married? Well, they want to get on welfare. "We had to!" That's what I would say routinely on the days we would cash our food stamps. We didn't have insurance, and Yvette was pregnant. Initially, there were five consecutive days of appointments before we got health-care insurance benefits. We would go to the welfare office, and they would ask the same series of questions, twice per month.

"Are you working?"

"No."

"Are you looking for work?"

"Yes."

"Where are you looking?"

"Everywhere."

"What kind of work are you attempting to do?"

"Anything."

"Have you considered the military?"

"No."

"Will you consider the military?"

"Yes."

It was the same barrage of questions over and over. Yvette, it didn't bother her. She had dealt with the welfare system before. When we finally got food stamps and health-care insurance, she was elated. She could eat chicken and cream-style corn. She could go to the store and buy slushies. (She was craving slushies!) For me, welfare was the most humiliating thing in the world. I refused to spend my food stamps at the grocery store near my home. We would go to the poorest neighborhood, where everybody uses food stamps. The first time we went to a store approximately 10 miles from our home, we ran into somebody we knew. And they wanted to talk, walk, and follow us to the checkout line. When we got there to pay with our food stamps there was the look of *"Oh!...I'm going to tell everybody at our church that you guys are on welfare."* You know the look. We loved the look of good Christian folks when they would stare at us when they realized that we were down and out. I wouldn't even let the words "…Oh! It is a temporary setback" come out of my mouth, because Yvette would quickly correct me and say, "I can find a job, but Babe can't find a job right now. Babe's looking. We'll find one eventually, right, Babe?"

Then she would look at me and I would say, "…Right!"

I was so defeated I did not know what to do. I was like the great athletes who suit up to play the game, only at the last minute, I would break a fingernail and decide I was too injured to go out there and play. I had lost my fight. Yvette was far more tenacious. Every job she applied for, she got. Everybody wanted to hire her; nobody wanted to hire me. It was an ongoing theme.

It was about that time when our eldest daughter was going to kindergarten that our financial troubles reached the breaking point (the word "divorce" was also uttered for the first time). We had expanded our family, and hoped that we would be able to support four kids in a way that God wanted. We had recently adopted two boys. We were shopping at K-Mart. It was unforgettable—that shopping trip. Yvette walked by one of the aisles and they were advertising a blue-light special with back-to-school stuff. She picked up a pink backpack and looked at me.

"I think we should get this pink backpack for LaTyia before she goes to school. I think LaTyia needs a backpack for kindergarten. Don't you agree, Mr. Rowlett?"

"Yvette, we are here to get essentials. We can't afford a pink backpack." Yvette was not in the mood to hear that; she stared at me and said, "One day I hope somebody will be able to afford to buy my daughter a pink backpack for school."

She turned abruptly and walked out of K-Mart, leaving me with all four of the kids standing there. I was shocked. I wanted to walk into that parking lot with my four kids, hand the kids over to her, and say "*It's over.*" We were at the point of no return. The kids looked at me. They all looked at their dad, and wanted to know why Mommy couldn't get the pink backpack. I remember leaving the cart filled with essentials sitting in K-Mart as we walked out the door. We got to the car, and I was ready to let her have it. And she was sitting there crying. Her eyes were red and bloodshot. She refused to acknowledge me or look at me as the kids got in. She was kind to them. "…Get in, kids. Get in, guys…just get in the car."

We all got into the car and drove home. I don't know if we spoke at all during the next two weeks: all over a pink backpack.

Things went from horrible to horrific. Bill collectors! When we were in college, credit-card companies would not just send us credit-card applications, they sent us credit-card applications already filled out. All we needed to do was fill in our Social Security number, age, birth date, and signature. We got credit cards by the mailbox-full. There was never an occasion where we couldn't go out and buy something on credit. We could stave off paying bills by getting a cash advance, depositing that to the bank, and paying the bills…knowing that one day we would be able to get jobs and pay off the cash advances. Until one day the phone rang and it was a bill collector. It was someone from Visa credit-card services, a representative from the Crocker Bank.

"Hello, Mr. Rowlett! This is a representative from Crocker Bank credit-card services and we are wondering if you are aware that your account is past due?"

"This is who?" I replied.

"A Crocker Bank credit-card representative, and I was wondering if you have a job because we would like to verify your employment."

"I don't have a job. I'm looking and I expect to be employed any day now."

"Mr. Rowlett, do you realize that you are 90 days in arrears on your payment?" Silence! I did not say a word. That was the first time I had ever talked to a bill collector. The person was very nice and very kind. We talked briefly about strategies to pay off the balance. They said we needed to discontinue using our credit card, as they had suspended it anyway. They wanted us to know that they were willing to be patient; but for no more than 30 days. When we couldn't make the next minimum payment, they turned us over to collections. Everybody (all the bill collectors) said that, and then everybody sent us to collections. Everybody! I didn't know what bad credit was. I didn't know what bill collectors were. However, soon thereafter the bills mounted, the collectors kept calling, and we were in red ink up to our eyeballs. Yvette would look at the bills and say, "Well, they can't get blood from a turnip! Nothing they can do about it until you get a job." She was working fairly regularly. I was working irregularly. She was bringing home a paycheck in addition to the welfare check that we would get. I felt I was not entitled to touch the money. Yvette handled all the money and the bills. She decided, and I agreed, that since we were not able to fulfill our financial obligations, it might be best just to try to eliminate every extra, until I got a job. We went into survival mode! We lived on Cream-Style Corn and Top Ramen; to this day I refuse to eat them.

Did I happen to share that, when we went into survival mode, I never suggested or thought that perhaps we should ask God for some wisdom or direction? It didn't dawn on me that perhaps paying tithes might have been God's plan for us. Eventually some of the debt was eliminated because we became more disciplined with our finances. However, we still did not regularly pay tithes. God promised that if we give him 10% of whatever we received that we would be blessed, and that we would not have room in our barns to contain the blessings that he would give us. It didn't dawn on me that perhaps the very thing that I was trying to achieve was the last thing that we needed to do: keep every penny. It didn't occur to me that we needed to give 10% of everything that we had to God. One day, when we were at Shiloh's Baptist Church, Yvette looked at me and suggested that we a pay a tithe, or give a one-time 10% offering. I remember curtly responding, "We can't afford it." Now, I look back and I know that we could not afford to keep doing what we were doing.

We continued to struggle with welfare for a long time until one day the phone rang. Some guy by the name of John Buck telephoned from Midtown Manor and offered me a job. We both had jobs. I was a counselor, and Yvette was a daycare center director. After weeks of considerable discussion, Yvette decided to start a home daycare business. It was called Yvette's Daycare. She resigned from her position as daycare center director, and opened her daycare business because she wanted to spend more time with the children. Her daycare business grew rapidly. Not working, being at home, and getting tax breaks for using your home as a business increased the income. Eliminating the extra gas expenses and being home with the kids was allowing us to get out of debt. I remember one day, during the holidays, we had over $500 in the bank. I remember telling Yvette, "We have $500 in the bank." We thought we were rich! We wanted to go splurge, go to the drive-in, or just do something. We were elated!

During that time, one of the husbands of the Bible-study sisters gave us a gift membership to become part of the Morris Ceurello World Evangelism Partnership Team. We said, "Thank you! And who the heck is Morris Ceurello?" Well, he is an evangelist. There was a conference that our friends, the Wilks, would attend every year in Anaheim, CA. Alfred Wilks (yes, same first name) and his family would drive down there; after a day at Disneyland, they would attend the conference and listen to world-renowned Christian speakers. These Christian speakers would encourage their family. We thought this was a great idea. Yvette and I thanked our friend Alfred profusely, and planned our own trip to Anaheim. By the time the day of the trip arrived, our bank account had swelled to $1,500. We were rich. It didn't matter that our credit rating had taken a severe beating over the years and that the only credit card we could get was one that required us to put $500 in a savings account as collateral. With that credit card and a bank balance of $1,500, we were comfortable taking our family to Anaheim. We were more than happy; we were elated and we joyously prepared for the trip. Then we got into our Toyota minivan and drove south to Anaheim.

It was during that conference that we were reintroduced to the concept of tithing. We arrived at the conference, were greeted by friends and other well-wishers who had gone to the church that we attended in Sacramento. We thought this was a small church service, but to our surprise there were thousands of people at the Anaheim convention center. We were practically sitting up in the rafters! We could see Morris Ceurello standing down on the stage; he looked like he was about two inches tall. We smiled, as we were just glad to be there. All six of us were sharing one room—the girls and Yvette in one bed, the boys and I in the other bed. That was all we could afford, but it didn't matter. We took shifts going to the bathroom and taking showers. I made sure that the boys used the bathroom last and then kept the fan on all night—you know why. We were having fun! We even got to go spend one day in Disneyland. That was a treat, and heck, we had $1,500 in the bank!

It was during one of the conference services that Morris Ceurello said, "Partners, I want you to give $750 to the ministry, and God told me He was going to bless your finances this year like never before." When Morris Ceurello said that, Yvette and I looked at each other…

$750? That was half of our nest egg! Yvette looked at me. She didn't say a thing. She was already giving money to another evangelist and I was thinking, *Why do we need to support two?* It took me about 10 seconds and then I asked her, "You want to do it?"

She said, "We've never given that much money to the church."

Both of us looked kind of giddy...kind of shocked! We were getting ready to give the Morris Ceurello Ministry $750—half of everything we had. The check was good; it didn't matter. I wrote the check out for $750 and gave it to her. We touched hands.

She said, "Okay, Babe, in Jesus' name."

We put it in the bucket and it was gone. We both sat there, waiting for a lightning bolt to strike us: no lightning. We waited for pennies from heaven: no pennies from heaven. Was I the only one who thought of reaching over and getting our money back out of that bucket? We gave all that money, half of what we had, to Morris Ceurello World Evangelism. It was the financial turning point in our lives—a point from which we never turned back. We became committed to tithing that day. From that point on, we gave 10% of everything that we received back to God.

Shortly after returning from the conference, we received an interesting piece of mail. It was from the American Express company. Early on in our marriage we had been offered an American Express card and foolishly agreed to open a credit account. We didn't know then that American Express cards do not have a preset limit. You just need to pay off your balance! Every Month! It didn't matter how large your balance. I ended up humbly cutting up the card. But now, after all these years, American Express was giving us a second chance. And, they said we were pre-qualified. Did this mean that all of our prayer and obedience to God's command about tithing had resulted in an immediate blessing? I don't know. It didn't matter. We filled out the American Express application and waited. Within a few days we had American Express cards—one for her and one for me. We stared at them. "...Ahhh!" We couldn't believe we had qualified for credit, just like everybody else. We were gleeful. I remember Yvette jumping up saying, "...Thank you!

Thank you! Thank you! Thank you! Thank you! Thank you, Jesus! Thank you, Jesus! I'm going out to shop."

I laughed. "No you are not."

"Babe, I'm going to shop. We can afford it."

I think that was about the last time I asked her how much she spent and on what. She went out shopping. She stayed gone for a long time, using her American Express card to buy whatever she wanted. She came back having spent a grand total of less than $100. I couldn't believe it. What I realized then, and I would realize for the rest of our marriage, Yvette was as thrifty and sensible as I was. She just didn't like the fact that I enforced my own brand of thriftiness and frugality on her. She had no desire to spend money on herself. She would buy things for our children and for her friends. She would always treat them to dinner. Having that American Express card became a symbol of freedom for us. It meant something. It meant that we had faith to endure the difficult financial times, and had earned our way back into good credit standing! That American Express card was symbolic of God's forgiving us for not tithing. It was an important part of our lives.

Years later, we were planning the trip of a lifetime. We were getting ready to travel to Israel! For our entire marriage, we had talked about traveling abroad to Israel. Yvette's father, Deddy, would occasionally dangle trips in front of us. He'd tell us, "You guys could save up $5,000 and go to Israel with me."

We would look at each other and say, "Why don't you ask us to save up $5 million? That would be easier." That year he said the same thing. But that year, because of God's mercy and grace, $5,000 didn't seem like an insurmountable amount of money. We chatted about it, kibitzed about it, kicked around a few pebbles, and finally she said, "Babe, let's do it. Let's go to Israel with Deddy. We can get Mom and Papa to go, we can make arrangements to have all of our friends keep the kids and go to Israel. A two-week vacation! Let's do it! Let's go to Israel."

It took me about a half day, and we decided. "*Okay, we'll go to Israel.*" We saved up the money, and we were on our way! We were thrilled. She had gone through several wonderful jobs, including working as a teacher, and was now an administrator with the State of California Department of Education. That little company that had offered me a job, Midtown Manor, had changed its name to Turning Point Community Programs and had grown tremendously. I was the Chief Operations Officer. We had just finished our Master's degrees together; hers was in Education, and mine was in Social Work. God was doing great things with our finances, and in our lives. Going to Israel was a culmination of years of prayers and hard work, of mistakes, of being hypocritical, and ultimately giving 10% of all we have received to God. She didn't stop there. She wouldn't stop there. She continued to help and bless other people. Going to Israel was her way of saying, "Wow, Lord, thank you!" Seeing Israel! It was the most amazing place we had ever been together. The fact that we were together made it even more special. Oh! It is important to note that we made that trip during the summer of 2001. After we returned, travel in America was changed forever on September 11, 2001.

That trip was followed years later by Yvette's trip to Africa. Africa represented the end of our financial frustrations. At that time, all of our children were grown, with the exception of Hannah. It was Hannah, Yvette, and I at home. Yvette had gotten together with some women at our church. They were sojourning to Africa to the country of Zambia; I called it her way of giving back. They were going to worship with women there. Her first battle with cancer was over; the doctor said she was in remission. She was thrilled to finally get to go to Africa! She would do amazing things while she was there. She would meet some incredible people. She, of course, adopted some of the kids in Africa, trying to put them into her suitcase, but that didn't work out for her. Hannah and I got to hear firsthand about her adventures in Africa. We hopped on an airplane and flew to London, meeting her at Heathrow Airport. I remember being on the airplane with my seven-year-old thinking, *We are flying to London, my seven-year-old and I. I thought only rich people did this, not Al and Yvette Rowlett.* I can remember getting off the plane at Heathrow. We didn't have a plan, we just trusted God knowing that we would find each other at one of the busiest airports in the world. London's Heathrow airport is immense. Hannah and I got off the plane, got on a train, and headed to the concourse where we assumed she would be. Well, what we knew about London was absolutely zero; but we did know something about airports. If there was an airport, somewhere inside the terminal was a Starbucks. So, Hannah and I headed to the nearest Starbucks in that terminal. Behold! As we were walking towards that Starbucks, I heard a voice yell, "There they are!" And I saw the most beautiful, skinny black lady run towards her daughter and me. I was thrilled to see her and she was thrilled to see me. I could hear her saying to her companions as she ran to us, "I told you they would find me. We didn't need a plan; the Holy Spirit worked it out for us." It was the way things were with us. We had learned to trust the Holy Spirit. We trusted that He would work things out for us.

We continued to give throughout the remainder of our marriage, unconditionally. Somebody couldn't buy diapers, Yvette would buy them; somebody couldn't pay their rent, we would pay it; and if somebody needed to use our car, we would loan it to them. Somebody needed to buy a car, we sold them our car at the lowest price possible. Yvette would remind me what it was like for us to be poor, of the difficulties that we had when we were in debt. She would tell me, "…Nobody reached out to help us. God never abandoned us." It was for "*better or worse*," "*until death part us*," God was always with us. We had survived those early years of welfare, bill collectors, no backpack, and no credit. She continued to be the first to volunteer to give away something, usually something monetary. She would remind me, "Babe, you got a good job. God has blessed you. We don't need to be stingy with our money. If somebody needs some help, we can help them. Remember, the Lord helped us; don't you ever forget that."

I'll never forget that. That mantra beats in my soul every day. I will never forget how she always gave unconditionally.

9

Wife or Patient?

"I thought I *almost* understood the impact my health has had on my husband, but, every day, I learn more about how he feels and the things he thinks. One day, he told me he missed having a wife versus a **patient**. I was glad he shared that with me, and it put me in check as to how I was acting. Was I acting like a patient with him, instead of a wife? That question would change my approach to life and my interactions with my husband.

"It is true that he spoiled me in every way. I could depend on him to do most things. Since we first got married, he always wanted to cook—for every meal, all the time! At first, I thought he just didn't like my style of cooking. It was not like Mom's cooking (southern style), and besides that, I was a vegetarian whereas he was definitely a "meat and potatoes" kind of guy. Vegetable spaghetti was not his idea of real food. So, for 28 years, he cooked most of the time.

"He has always been very involved in the kids' activities. When I signed my oldest son (he was four at the time) up for soccer, Alfred was the one who ended up coaching for 12 years. Yes, two practices and one game a week, for ten weeks of every year. Coach Al was the best, and he was totally committed to it.

"He was PTA president at the kids' school, and did whatever needed to be done. After the sarcoidosis diagnosis, he went on the field trips with the kids—whether it was a two-hour field trip or a week-long camping adventure. If I couldn't do it, for whatever reason, he was right there. He has been the best father and husband. Oh, we have had our differences, and we don't always agree on how things should be handled, but I could never say he has ever mistreated me.

"Now, for the first time, I heard a hint of '*You could help out a little more*' in his voice. I have always worked, in the home or out, and I have always tried to support him. But, the truth is he has been the super supporter when it comes to the kids and the household…time for me to step up.

"What a time to have to step up! I am facing yet another biopsy, and no one knows what the result of that will be. God knows, but He hasn't told me yet. I recently stopped working and am on medical leave. Yes, I am home, but for the first couple weeks, taking the kids to school and picking them up seemed like a lot. Yes, while they are gone, most of my days have been spent filling out paperwork and doing chores that were way overdue in the house. Cooking? Yes, I've cooked dinner, but very simple meals so far, just to get us through the day. The kids are fine with whatever, but Alfred, he is always fasting and praying. So I have not had to feel the pressure of cooking for him until he made that statement.

"One day, he did come home and ask me what I had been doing all day. I was annoyed by the question, and I'm sure my face showed it. I named about five things, and he changed the subject. But his question stuck with me.

"Am I doing enough? I go out of my way to prove to the rest of the world that I don't have a disease and I am not sick, but do I act differently with him? The truth is that I like for him to take care of me. I like when he cooks dinner, when he makes me a cup of hot tea just because, and when he asks me what I would like for breakfast and prepares it. But wow, Lord, the time has come for change.

"God has called him to do so many things right now, and my role is changing. I now need to be more supportive of him and his needs. He can't sit around waiting on me anymore. Yes, I need to wait on him, even though he is not used to that, and, once he realizes he can trust me, I believe he will allow me to be his help-mate in a different role. It's somewhat scary, but I believe this is the path God has chosen for me, and I will enjoy moving into it."

***

"Lord God,

I thank you for not giving up on me, but for expanding my territory—no matter what the doctors are saying. You, Lord, know the outcome. I know that I trust You and I know that I am not perfect, but that You love me anyway. I know that if You tell me to do something, You will equip me to do it. I may not know how to support my husband in this new way, but You, Lord God, know exactly what he needs and You know how and what I must do. Help me, Lord, to follow the lead of Your Precious Holy Spirit, read Your Word, and seek good, Godly advice as I move into this new role.

"Yes Lord, I have been a faithful wife for a long time, and I have provided for my husband. But this is new for me, and although I don't know everything to expect, help me to be open to Your will. Help me to move forward, with no complaining when I don't understand, standing firm, knowing that I am doing Your will. Lord, I ask you to help me be a good wife to my husband and not a patient. In Jesus' name, Amen."

10

Sad Days

"I decided today that what the Lord wants me to do is share my ups and downs, my good days and bad days. Just because I am a Christian does not mean I will not have moments of sadness, but, because I am a Christian, it means they will be just that: mere moments of sadness to be followed by a lifetime of joy.

"I refuse to spend one more day wallowing in self-pity and wondering '*Why me? Why not me?*' I am a strong Christian woman who loves the Lord with all my heart and soul. I honestly believe what is written in the Bible about how much Jesus loves me and that He cares about my every need. I have believed in Jesus as long as I can remember. I may not have always acted like it, but I do believe He is who He says He is, the Christ, Son of God.

"If He cares about my every need, then He cares when I am sad or lonely. He doesn't want me to feel that way, so if I know and believe that, and still do feel sad and lonely, then it is my issue, not Jesus. He has given me instructions to call on His name; I just need to do it.

"So, today I decided that yes, I would much rather be healthy, but each of us has our cross to bear and this is mine. I don't want to pass it on to anyone else; I want to do what God wants me to do with this cross—bear it. Two years ago, when I was diagnosed with cancer, I cried for a little bit and then I decided that was not going to get me anywhere. I encouraged myself in the Lord. I reminded myself of what the Word of God says about crying out to Him when we are in need. I cried out to Him and He comforted me. I never thought throughout the time of chemo and radiation that cancer would kill me. As a matter of fact, while I was in the hospital and the doctors had pretty much given up on me, I told my husband that if the Lord called me home he should not put in the obituary that I died from complications from cancer. I believe the Lord spoke to me soon after I was diagnosed and told me that cancer would not take my life; I was not going to let cancer get the credit for my death. Well, as it was to be, I did not die that day. I know without a doubt that the intercessory prayer and obedience of my husband was the reason the Lord kept me (that is another story). I believe that God will tell us something and make a promise to us, but we have a responsibility in that promise as well.

"Here we are, two years later. The doctors have told me that there are several tumors on my lungs, and now they have found a mass on my bladder. Wow! I was diagnosed with pulmonary sarcoidosis many years ago—15 years ago, to be exact. I have experienced many surgical procedures and tried lots of different medications. For the past five years, my doctor and I have agreed on Prednisone, Plaquenil, and cough syrup with codeine to get through the days. It has been helping, and I have been able to work and function pretty well. While I know the medicine is important, the prayers are what sustain me daily.

"There are days when it hurts terribly just to breathe; it seems I am supposed to just accept the pain and continue to be thankful to be alive. I was told by several doctors five years ago that I wouldn't live for another two years. The years have come and gone, and I am still here and still alive. I have put in a request for a lung transplant twice now and both times I was turned down. As a matter of fact, my main pulmonary specialist usually sees me and just asks me how I am and what would I like him to do. He won't admit to being a Christian or believing in God, but he will admit that I have something going on with the Lord. I do! This is not about medicine or disease: this is a spiritual battle.

"Pulmonary Sarcoidosis and cancer are horrible diseases to experience. I remember asking the Lord why I had to go through it. I also asked the Lord to help me to learn everything I needed to learn during this experience so I wouldn't have to repeat the lessons. Yes, this week, I thought, *Wow, Lord! Did I not get a lesson the last time?* When I was first diagnosed with cancer, my husband fasted one day a week for the entire time. He would go on prayer walks, and he read the Word daily. He is a mighty man of God but, before the cancer, he was not as faithful with reading, praying, and ministering to others. He made the commitment and he asked the Lord to spare my life. God did! He has not stopped fasting for one day a week and his prayer walks have increased. He studies the Word daily and prayer is continuously in his mouth. He leads a young men's Bible study, and I cannot say enough about how much he gives of himself.

"My husband sits on several boards, and they all keep him busy. God is using him in a mighty way, and I do not want to be a distraction to the work God has him doing. My husband is closer to the Lord than he has ever been; he is on fire for Jesus. He is involved so much in the community and loving every minute of it. I am so very proud of him and I don't want him to miss anything. Good things came out of me having cancer. Yet, I don't care; I do not want to go through it again!

"My daughter was married last Saturday, and I actually found out about the tumors on the lung two days before her wedding. I decided that that news was only for the Lord and me. I did not want the focus at the wedding or anytime during the weekend to be on me, but only on my oldest daughter and her very special day. It was very special.

"I remember years ago, when I was first diagnosed with pulmonary sarcoidosis, my daughter was young, about 12 years old, and I thought about dying and what that would mean to her. I asked the Lord to spare my life and allow me to be there when my (then!) two girls were married. I wanted to spend their wedding days with them and watch my husband walk them down the aisle. As it is, one daughter was married last year and the other this year. I thank the Lord that I was able to be there for both of them.

"My oldest, who just married, asked if her father and I would walk her down the aisle instead of just her father. I didn't like that request because I remembered my prayer. I didn't want to tell her that, so I agreed to walk with him. As things began to unfold, on the night before the wedding, my son went to my husband and said he didn't think it was right that we both walked her down. He said that is for a father to do—to walk her down and hand her over to her new husband. We agreed, and the next day he walked her down. We never told her we were changing the plans. She was surprised and very accepting.

"I am saddened to think that I had asked the Lord to witness their marriages. Now they were married, so did that mean that the Lord had fulfilled his promise, and that He could call me home? I was concerned, especially after just hearing the new diagnosis of tumors in my lungs.

"Another interesting thing happened that also made me sad. When I had cancer two years ago, I kept feeling the need to clean out my closet. I didn't want my husband to clean it out because he believes in tossing out everything and I am more of a packrat. He wanted it cleaned out, and I just did not have the energy to clean it. I kept thinking about cleaning that closet. One day, I started cleaning it, and a chill came over me. I thought, *If I clean out this closet, then the Lord may call me home, because there is nothing else in this house that Alfred cannot take care of himself.* So I stopped; I never cleaned out my closet.

"I heard a pastor preach once about how God needs us, and that as long as God needs us and we are doing something to advance His Kingdom of God, he will let us remain here and work. I was getting kind of nervous now. He didn't need me to clean out anything else in the house (although the garage always needs something) and now I had seen my girls get married off. My job was in good hands; someone else could take over if I had to leave permanently. I thought, *Wow, is the Lord setting me up to leave here?*

Not too long ago, my husband told me that the Lord spoke to him and told him that he should treasure every day with me. Uh oh, that sounds like lights out! On top of that, I have been having this reoccurring dream about a very large house with lots of rooms, and I am constantly fixing this house for children and the children keep coming. I was telling my husband about this dream one day and he said, "... That sounds like heaven: a beautiful mansion with many rooms and lots of children." He asked if he was there, or if there was a kitchen. I said, "No!" I could not remember him in any of the dreams, but I felt comfortable, like he just wasn't home yet. He continues to think the dream is about heaven. I loved that dream until he said that; I immediately stopped talking about dreams with him.

"I had been talking about retiring from my job for about nine months. The week or so before the wedding, I went in and told them I was going to retire. I told them on Thursday, and then on Friday, went in to sign the papers and changed my mind. No job—no one to share with or minister to all day? That was a sad day. If I'm not sharing or ministering all day, why be here?

"I left the job that day and recalled that in January of that year, I had the privilege of going to the Presidential Inauguration in Washington, DC. I was so excited! I would see the first black president and a couple that I admired. My father was able to get tickets, and off we went. We even went to one of the balls while we were there! I was so thankful to the Lord for such an opportunity. What I didn't expect was bitter cold, and yes, I became quite ill after standing outside for several hours. I came back to California and ended up in the hospital for almost a week with pneumonia. My already scarred lungs had taken a real beating. Oh yeah! I failed to mention my son had also decided to get married. Babe and I did not know that was their intent. The wedding was planned a few days after we returned from Washington, DC. Only, I was in the hospital. The wedding took place at my house; I was on the speaker phone lying in the hospital bed listening. It was a sad day for me. It was sad for several reasons, but one of them was the realization that a wedding could go on without me. I was the organizer in the family, but now I understood that they did not need me to organize things. Life was going on without me.

"Yes, I have had many examples of how life will go on without me. That is a sad feeling for me. I mean, I want life to go on, but doesn't my life mean anything to anyone? Recently, we had a Bible study at my house and a lady was there who had been battling cancer. That night, she talked about how she wasn't afraid to die. We were studying Esther and how she was in the king's palace for '*such a time as this.*' She was able to influence the king and save her people—an orphaned child, now a queen. Well, the very next day, that friend went to lunch, had a massive stroke, and went on to be with the Lord a couple days later.

"That had a great impact on me. I have faced the idea of death for many years and I didn't think I was afraid. I truly believe she was not afraid of dying. When I went to the hospital room to see her the next evening, I was comforted by the Holy Spirit. It was like she was lying there having a conversation with someone, just waiting for her turn to enter heaven. There was a peace about her. Even looking at her, I experienced that peace...but I did not want to join her.

"That night I had a conversation with the Lord about raising my eight-year-old daughter. I remember when I first adopted her that I asked the Lord if I was too sick to raise another child. I told the Lord if He wanted me to raise her, I needed Him to spare my life. I felt total peace that I was doing what God wanted me to do. She was a year old then, and I felt too old and too sick to try to raise a baby. The Lord comforted me completely, and I knew what I was doing was right.

"So, now I sit here, eight years later, asking God, '*What is going on? She is only eight years old and she needs her mother!*' Deep down I know it does not have to be me. She is God's child, and He can keep her without me. That is a sad feeling for me. I want to be here to raise her, see her walk down the aisle with her dad, and watch him hand her over to her husband. That is so special; it will still be special without my being there."

"Dear Lord,

What does the future hold? I think I want to know. I know one day I will leave this earth and be with You. But, when is the right time? Only You know, Lord. I don't want to rush things by my disobedience, but I don't want to extend things either. I want to be aligned with You, Lord, so I am ready when that moment comes. No shock, no being unprepared, but ready and at peace. Teach me, Lord, to trust You more, to draw even closer to You and teach me to pour into the lives of those here on earth. Teach me to be the Christian example that You want me to be while I am here.

"Help me, Lord, not be afraid. Help me to accept the cross that You have for me. No whining, no complaining; more joy than sadness. Help me to not 'fall into' any trap the devil may have laid for me. Teach me how to walk over or around them and complete the work You have for me. Sadness for a moment; but joy for hours. In Jesus' Name, Amen."

11

The Road Home Has Potholes

As Yvette said, we began 2009 like two million–plus other people: shivering and huddled together alongside the Reflection Pool in Washington, DC. It was unlike any other event; we were there to witness the first African American in the history of the United States being sworn in as president. Unbeknownst to both of us, it was the beginning of the end of our marriage and of her life on earth. She planned every detail of the trip, starting in November, the day after the nation elected Barack Obama as president of the United States. She telephoned her father and asked, "Deddy, are you going?"

It was a short conversation, as the next thing Yvette did was to sit at her computer, rubbing her upper lip gently as she began planning our trip to Washington, DC. I was all for it, provided she take the necessary precautions to guard against illness…especially pneumonia. We knew that the risk of overexposure in the oftentimes chilly air of Washington, DC, in January was great. We wanted to make sure that her health was not compromised.

"Babe, don't worry, the Lord will take care of me!"

That was her theme song.

"I am going to make it" was the chorus.

Well, although that was how November began, it ended far differently. Our son Tyler had recently telephoned informing us that he was going to be coming to Sacramento. We were excited, but cautious, as most of Tyler's decisions were exclusively his own. He also informed us that a young lady that we both knew would be accompanying him. Moreover, that they had been dating for some time, and had decided to discontinue the long-distance nature of their relationship, move to Arizona, and live together.

"Oh, my! Babe, what do you think?"

I was less diplomatic. "Tyler, do you care what the Lord has to say about the two of you living together?"

"Yes and no!" Tyler was quick to inform us. "We just want to be together!"

I replied, "Oreo cookies want to be together, but they are separated by the cream filling!" It was not my best and brightest response.

Yvette was far more thoughtful and direct. "Well, munchkin, I guess you just have to make it on your own, because your dad and I cannot support that at all. We love you and we think this is a terrible decision."

She looked at me; I was poised to snap off a brief oral dissertation, as she began shaking her head franticly.

"No!" I snorted like a whale that had just come up for air. We hung up the telephone, and I was met with, "…Well let's examine this before we respond."

I was waiting for a fresh insight to hit me, but there was nothing forthcoming. I went to bed. We disagreed throughout the night regarding my desire to take Tyler out of the Rowlett Family Trust.

That weekend, Tyler showed up at about noon in a red car driven by his girlfriend. They came to the door in unison, and Tyler said, "Mommy and Daddy, we are moving to Arizona."

Tyler sounded like he actually knew what he was doing. His girlfriend had a precocious child who was almost two years old. She was with them. My daughter, LaTyia, who was staying with us in the Casita, was fascinated by the child. Tyler and his girlfriend wanted no part of my conversation. It was apparent that this was intended to be a short visit.

The red car…it was a study in how not to move to Arizona. It was filled to the brim with stuff—all kinds of stuff! It had tires as bald as a billiard ball. Honestly, the fuzz on the billiard ball exceeded the tread on at least two of the tires. Yvette finally got them to agree to come in the house, much to my consternation.

"He'll be okay; you guys aren't listening to us anyway."

Yvette played with the baby. After almost an hour, we prayed. I once again, but less vociferously, tried to get them to change their minds and consider marriage. "No! You are not going to control our lives."

I just stopped talking.

"Tyler, drive safely, we love you and disagree with you," Yvette responded politely.

We walked them to the car when I noticed, "Oh you have a flat tire!"

Tyler's girlfriend replied, "I just bought those tires!"

"You purchased bald tires? Why did you do that?" I was at my cross-examining best. Yvette redirected me. "Why don't you and the baby come in, and let them change the tire?"

Tyler immediately opened the trunk: it looked like a scene from *The Beverly Hillbillies* sitcom, and Tyler was starring as Mr. Clampett. He had to remove everything from that trunk to get to the spare tire. I was chuckling so much, Tyler stopped and asked if I wanted to wait inside. I agreed, as I was not helping him.

It was, unfortunately, an omen of things to come. After retrieving the spare, another tire began to simultaneously deflate. No kidding! It was going flat! What a miraculous event; as we all stood there it soon became apparent that Tyler was not driving anywhere. More importantly, there was the girlfriend and the child. After a huddle, Yvette and I decided to buy them a new set of tires. Why? I don't know! It was like the Holy Spirit wanted us to be kind. We reinflated the tires and drove to the tire shop. We knew God was trying to tell them something about living together, but they wanted no part of God's message. They were appreciative that we would buy them tires so they could begin their trek to Arizona, but they wanted no part of us or God's message. The girlfriend agreed to follow me to the tire shop and depart immediately for Arizona after the tires were installed. The tires were purchased for the *"meager price of four hundred dollars."* Yvette was amused when I telephoned and told her how much they cost. As we departed the tire establishment, I looked in the rear-view mirror and noticed the girlfriend's car was stalling. She was following me at the time. I pulled over, and when I got out of my car I could see that Tyler's girlfriend was weeping uncontrollably. The car had died. After several attempts to restart the vehicle, it was apparent there were additional problems. We had the car towed to the house, put Tyler on a plane back to Arizona, and agreed to let the girlfriend move in with us. What boundaries? We didn't have any when it came to doing God's work.

"Well, we're going to Washington, DC," Yvette explained. "We are going to Washington, DC!"

"Okay," I agreed. We moved the girlfriend and the baby into our spare bedroom and planned for the holidays. Little did we know that it was going to be the last Christmas we would spend together on earth. I often reflect on how 2008 ended and ponder, *Would we do it the same way if we had known she was going to die?* Would we have done all the same things in 2009? Consider, and you decide.

January 2009, Yvette was not feeling well when we departed for Washington, DC, but she had painstakingly planned every detail of our trip. We left prepared for Siberia; we even packed Pampers for the trip to the mall in Washington, DC! Did I mention we were going to join two or three million of our closest friends as spectators at the inauguration of the first African American president in the history of the country? What a great experience! Unfortunately, it was so very cold. Exposure to the bitter elements resulted in Yvette becoming seriously ill. I suspected she was not well, yet she constantly said, "Babe, I'm okay!"

No problem; we had a car with a driver, for the outrageously low price of seven hundred and fifty dollars for four days. Or so we thought…Yvette had made a slight miscalculation: it was that much **per** day. We left for Washington, DC, not expecting that we would return to Sacramento three thousand dollars poorer. Yvette was furious that I had consented to pay the driver. I calmly responded, "…My wife is worth a lot more than seven hundred and fifty dollars per day. God obviously concealed this bit of information. If you had known, you would have insisted that we catch the subway train." Having a car afforded Yvette the opportunity to escape the weather while the rest of us stood outside and nearly froze to death; she watched the inauguration from the warm backseat of a minivan.

Returning home to Sacramento, Yvette was more inclined to be honest. "Babe, I can't breathe!" Yvette was on oxygen therapy and still could not breathe. As soon as the plane landed I said, "Okay! Let's go to the hospital." Off to the hospital, only to frighten a student nurse with a pulse rate so high and an oxygen level so low the poor girl almost passed out in the examination room. She ran out of the examination room to her supervisor. "I think she is very sick!"

Yvette was immediately admitted; she was hospitalized for one week with pneumonia and a partial pneumothorax (the medical term for a collapsed lung). A couple of days later, while Yvette was in the hospital, Tyler and his girlfriend, who remained a guest in our home until we returned from Washington, DC, got married in our family room. Yvette listened to the ceremony from her hospital bed via a friend's cellular telephone. Yvette was discharged a few days after they left for Arizona.

In February, Yvette tried to return to work without oxygen. It was impossible. For the first time, I discerned she was frightened. She tried a portable oxygen tank; it was woefully inadequate. No problem; her supervisor told her that she could work from home. At home, we had three large liquid oxygen tanks at the ready in the hallway, and by the end of February Yvette was oxygen dependent twenty-four hours per day.

March of 2009 was the first time I acknowledged that she was extremely ill and perhaps closer to a crisis than I had ever wanted to believe. It was my fiftieth birthday. We had a party, which was attended by lots of friends and family, and my not-so-proud wife walked around attached to her oxygen. She was adamant that she would not be defined by her diseases. Yet, on that day, she could not entertain without the help of the oxygen.

In April, Yvette applied for and was granted temporary disability. She essentially stopped working. During the month of May we celebrated her fifty-first birthday by agreeing to allow my nephew to relocate from Denver, Colorado, to Sacramento and live with us.

"Permanently?"

"Yes, Babe, I guess Culese [my nephew] is going to live with us."

"He is seventeen years old!" I exclaimed, hoping that would dissuade her.

"Yes!" she said calmly. "…He is going to live with us."

She was barely alive, and here we were agreeing to take care of another child.

"Why?" I would wonder aloud. The answer was obvious: God wanted us to.

At the end of the month of May, once school was out, we decided to drive to Arizona. We had received several distressing telephone calls from Tyler implying that things were not going well. Once again, we decided the direct approach was the best alternative. We drove all night to Arizona, Yvette, Hannah, Culese, and I, to meet with Tyler. His bride had moved out, and it was obvious they had been fighting. I told Tyler that God wanted him to love his wife and child, not fight with them. Unfortunately, Tyler was having none of it. We made one last unsuccessful attempt to get them help, but they were recalcitrant. We recommended other relatives and close friends in Arizona as an option, but they were not willing to seek their help. It was a difficult time. What we did not know was that would be the last time Tyler would see his mom alive.

When we returned to Sacramento, our eldest son, Kirkland, asked if he could move back home. That decision required a lot of thought and prayer. After several jobs and apartments, he was in a somewhat desperate circumstance. It was one of those things that seemed to happen to us a lot: there would be a knock at the door, and a few days later someone would be living with us. We prayed a lot about this decision, wanting to give Kirkland the message of love without condoning any behaviors that might have been offensive to our Lord. We agreed in prayer! Kirkland moved into the Casita. Yvette was very skeptical. "Babe, I am not sure this is the right thing to do. He is not going to find a job living in the Casita!" she would often exclaim. We would look at each other. "God's love for Kirkland Mario." She would always shake her head and pray for his future.

June began with us receiving a collect call from the Meracupa County Jail; it was Tyler.

"Hi Daddy and Mommy…I am in jail." the voice was somber and recognizable. Tyler was in jail, something neither of us ever condoned.

"Tyler, you know better. What were you thinking?"

"Mommy, she was—"

"It does not matter; we did not raise you to be…"

There was a long silence. "Mommy, I am sorry."

Incredulity meets reality. There was nothing we could do, or were going to do, at that time. We were stunned and saddened that our son was in jail. Would he soon be a convicted felon? We prayed and cried a lot that day. It was the last thing that we wanted for any of our children! She would periodically ask me over the course of the next 90 days, and countless collect calls, if I was planning a trip to Arizona. I would smile at her and say, "…I am not going to leave you."

Did I happen to mention that our eldest daughter, LaTyia, was living with us during the summer? LaTyia was planning her wedding during those months. She was getting married in September. Her fiancé, Kyiame, and his son were residing in a home that they had purchased. The two of them relocated from Florida and were living in Sacramento, but LaTyia would stay with us until their wedding. Yvette loved it! LaTyia would come into our room at night, and they would talk for hours. Yvette would smile and say, "She is a good teacher, Mr. Rowlett."

I agreed. "Yes! The Lord has blessed us."

Kimberly and Jesse were in a slightly different place. The first year of marriage "ughs"! There is no other way to describe it. You get married, divorced, apologize, date, and fall in love all in the same morning that first year of marriage. Yvette loved talking to Kimberly in the morning. She would call me and describe in great detail what I needed to do and what I needed to pray about. It was amazing. She and Kimberly had a sort of synergy that was not defined as much by their mother/daughter relationship as by their personalities. They were alike and different in many ways. They could have an hour-long chat in fifteen minutes. They were both excited that the summer was going to end with LaTyia's wedding in September.

I failed to mention something: back in the month of May of 2009 while I was at a men's retreat for church, I received an interesting e-mail. It read: "*Al, I am planning on resigning from my position as Elk Grove Unified School District (EGUSD) Trustee for area 7. I hope you might be interested. Sincerely, your friend, Brian Myers.*" For over a decade, Yvette and I had prayed and talked about leadership and politics. I thought it would never happen; in fact, I had given up. She, on the other hand, was constantly cajoling me to run for office. It had become almost abusive. "I am going to die before you get elected. Some other woman is going to be there with you when you are getting sworn in. I am going to tell the Lord to make it rain or something on just you!" For my part, I would remind her that swearing-in ceremonies are held indoors. Finally, the day had come, just as the Lord had promised. I came home from the Men's Advance, read the e-mail, and then went for a long prayer walk, after which I cried. I remember thanking God, and kissing Yvette. She was elated, but I was nervous.

June and July were a blur of activity, planning for EGUSD consideration and nightly budget discussions related to the wedding. As much as she loved it, wedding planning sapped Yvette of energy; it had a similar effect on our checking account. I was frustrated, but she was happy.

"Babe, it's okay! The Lord is going to take care of us."

"Yvette, I do not want to live on bread alone so my daughter can be happily married!" I would reply constantly, but she was unwavering.

"We have the money, and Tyia has been a good daughter. What more do you want? We have everything we need. Fine, Mr. Rowlett, if you are that concerned I will go back to work."

Check and mate! She knew I did not want her to go back to work. I wanted her alive and with me. I would snarl and head into the other room, but I was always glad that I lost those arguments.

The EGUSD school board application process was very straightforward: provide us with your completed application and one living male child, preferably your firstborn. "Just one?" we joked. It wasn't that we were intimidated. At least, *she* was not intimidated. I was nervous as I drove up to the Elk Grove Unified School District's administrative offices that day. She was happy as a lark, sitting in the passenger seat. We parked the car and she began with this prayer: "Lord, bless Babe! He can do it if you give him Your strength. In Jesus' name, Amen."

"Yvette, where is your oxygen?"

"I don't need it today, Babe!"

She did not bring her portable oxygen; I was too wrapped up in my own head to even notice. They called the candidates in one at a time. My turn: three-minute introduction, eleven minutes for questions and answers, and one minute for wrap-up, all totaling fifteen minutes. We had gone over it several times, and had prayed for this opportunity for years. I remember introducing myself, and my closing comments. When it was over, I walked out of the board chambers and did not look at Yvette. I waited along with eight other candidates; their professions included: a doctor, former school district superintendent, prison warden, and a couple of very active parents in the school community. After almost two hours, the eight candidates were summoned back into the board chamber. The president, Mr. Lugg, greeted each of us as we returned; I glanced at Yvette for a sign. She winked at me in that way which always made me feel complete as a man. She also smiled so broadly I thought her face was going to fall off. Mr. Lugg made his proclamation: "We would like to thank each of the candidates for submitting an application and going through the process. After careful deliberation, it is clear one candidate was superior. At this time, I would like to announce that the trustees for the Elk Grove Unified School District have selected Alfred 'Al' Rowlett as the new trustee for area seven." I was calm; she just smiled. I went over to Yvette and kissed her. She was so proud of her husband.

"I love you, Babe!" She whispered it in my ear softly and I looked at her: all that courage and strength, there as always. I was emotionally spent; she was floating on a cloud.

I thought that the summer would slowly fizzle out, Yvette would retire, I would work for Turning Point Community Programs and the Elk Grove School District, and LaTyia would get married. That would be it for the rest of our lives.

That night, Yvette asked me a question.

"Babe, what about intimacy?"

She hated the fact that the diseases robbed our marriage of this. I did not respond; I was not willing to answer the question.

"You wait; I am going to get better. And since you think I'm so cute anyway, Mr. Rowlett, you won't be able to resist me."

I looked at her and almost spontaneously started crying in front of her.

"Babe, it is okay. The Lord is going to heal me, watch! He is. He promised." We did not talk about intimacy anymore for the rest of our married life together.

August came and went like a flurry. It was September. LaTyia was getting married. Yvette was home; she took over taking the kids to school, and I was working. I thought, This could work. Things were settling down. Although Kirkland was living in the Casita, Tyler was still incarcerated, and I was standing in a briefing room in Los Angeles, CA, when I received a telephone call.

"Babe, I am at Kaiser and I am in pain!"

"Yvette!" I exclaimed. "…What happened?" My thoughts began to race. She was in pain, and I was in Los Angeles, CA.

She interrupted, "But the doctor said my lung is reinflating. All this time we thought it was cancer, or something worse, and it is my lung. Renita is with me. Don't worry, okay, Babe?"

What could I say? "Okay." I ended the telephone call. I actually began to have fantasies, standing in an LA County briefing room, about Yvette returning to work. I envisioned the Lord healing her like one of those great champions of the faith. She was on TV, in my mind, sharing her testimony with everyone. Upon my return to Sacramento, I was challenged; the reality was so different. She was very sick and maybe dying. I just wanted to get home and see her. When I arrived at home, I was the recipient of a two-hour nonstop recount of the day:

"And the Lord reinflated my lung. The doctor wanted to stick a tube into my chest and I said, '*Take an X-ray.*' The lung was healing itself. Women from the church came to the hospital and prayed for me, and I told them that the Lord was healing me. That's good, right, Babe? The doctor said, 'Your lung is reinflating on its own!'

"I told the doctor, 'The Lord is reinflating my lung!'"

That night, after a flurry of telephone calls and visits from the kids, falling asleep I had a fascinating dream. Yvette was in my dream, and I heard her say "Babe, I am okay!" on three separate occasions. I woke up early that morning and walked outside, pacing, pleading and praying aloud around the pool. I knew at that moment that Yvette was going to die. I would never tell her the truth regarding that dream.

In September we had the wedding; it was a culminating event for Yvette. Our eldest daughter was getting married! Yvette and I were supposed to walk her down the aisle together. Neither of us seemed to care that the aisle was barely wide enough to accommodate two people, let alone three. At the last minute on the day before the wedding, my son Trey came over to me and said, "Sir, the Lord told me that you are supposed to walk Tyia down the aisle, not you and Mommy."

I glared at him and said, "Are you sure the Lord told you that, Trey?"

"Yes, sir!"

I failed to mention that, I was only lukewarm about the marriage, whereas Yvette was thrilled. I was wrong and she was right, of course. At the time Trey made his prophetic statement, I was convinced Yvette would resist any last-minute changes.

"Yvette, the Lord told Trey to tell me that I should walk LaTyia down the aisle, and not the two of us."

"Okay, Babe. Someone else can escort me in."

I was dumbfounded. That was it? She had spent our entire marriage challenging all of my last-minute changes or alterations to her plans. No argument, just an "Okay, Babe." As if she knew this was what the Lord wanted. And the wedding was a tremendous success. She finished the day depleted, utilizing the portable oxygen with each step. After the ceremony, all she said to me was, "I am happy I got to live and see both my daughters get married."

Disneyland!!! It was early in the month of October; vacation was an afterthought, a brief interruption, or another one of Yvette's last-minute, end-of-life requests. In any case, we drove off to Anaheim, CA, in October of 2009 because she wanted to take Hannah to Disneyland. I drove all the way. I looked at her constantly, my thoughts related to the dream; things started darting back and forth in my head. How and why was this going to happen? It was, as always, up to God. I continually prayed for a miracle. Oftentimes, my thoughts would drift off in the car as I pretended I was by myself. I would start to cry out to God and then gather myself. Prior to us driving to Disneyland, Yvette had undergone a full-body scan and several blood tests to determine what was wrong. She was getting weaker, not stronger, with each passing day. She was not able to drive the kids to school or pick them up any longer. But, we put it out of our minds. We were going to Disneyland, the happiest place on earth! At Disneyland we were going to be happy, for Hannah, one last time. It was going to be great.

Yvette made one trip to the Disneyland infirmary, where she stayed for three hours. It was a place I had never seen at Disneyland. Yvette was so happy, she sent us off to play while she rested. We of course refused to leave, pretending to marvel at the hospital. The people on the hospital staff were as friendly as the people on the grounds of Disneyland. Of course, while she slept, we all watched her and prayed.

We finished our day at Disneyland and returned to the hotel. Her oxygen usage was still at the maximum level her portable tank could tolerate. I was considering aborting our trip for a mad dash back to Sacramento.

"Nope, Mr. Rowlett! I have to see my brother, Jimmy, and his son, Little Jimmy."

She was insistent. I gave in, and we had a great visit. She loved being there. Yvette deeply loved her brother and nephew. Her love for her older brother Jimmy grew out of a lifetime of unrelenting support and appreciation. After visiting for several hours, she felt so good she wanted to drive back. I thought this was a good sign, until she drove about fifteen minutes and had to stop. I looked at Yvette as she tried to conceal her thick blanket of tears from me.

"I can't drive anymore."

That was the last time she drove a car. I took over, we kind of joked about her driving skills, after which there was that long period of silence. I think she knew then, as I did, that she was going to die soon.

October ended painfully, like a scab that never heals because it continually gets ripped off. It was October 30, 2009, and we were meeting with the oncologist. He had the results of the scan. He looked at us and said, "I understand that you folks like to get the facts."

"Yes!" we replied, curious about his introduction.

"I have reviewed the scan and the cancer is back. It has metastasized to your bladder, lymph nodes, and lungs. As a result, you will die in 6–12 months." Silence. No one spoke for several awkward seconds. We looked at each other, and the doctor, obviously uncomfortable with the silence, asked, "Are you okay with that?"

"Babe," she said, "…are you okay?"

I looked at her, and we leaped up, grabbed each other, and stood there weeping like little children.

12

The Word "No"

November 2009 began with us trying to tell our children that Yvette was going to die in six to twelve months. Each child was discouraged and grief-stricken. We all agreed that she would go to the Mayo Clinic in Arizona during the month of December. We were in agreement that Renita would accompany her, as Culese and Hannah were still in school and I needed to stay home with them. There were the other dreaded but necessary communication details: parents, friends, and co-workers would all be told the horrible news. It felt like we had to tell the entire world about Yvette's condition. We debated and argued for hours about this. Finally, we agreed that we needed to say something... only what? After numerous unproductive attempts, the need to communicate something to the people in our lives who we cared about was imperative. We decided; it read as follows:

> *Hello everyone,*
>
> *We would like to begin by thanking you for your prayers and words of encouragement. We met with the oncologist recently, and the news is not what we hoped for. He said the cancer is back and has spread to other parts of Yvette's body, including the lungs, backbone, and some lymph nodes. There is no treatment plan at this point. God has been faithful throughout this process and we*

continue to trust Him completely. We ask for your prayers, know-
ing that God's healing hand is what we need and believe in. We
appreciate all the acts of love that have been extended to our fam-
ily and we will continue to keep you updated on Yvette's progress.
Please feel free to e-mail us; calling is fine, but it does get a bit
overwhelming.

Daniel 3:17–18 (NKJV): "If we are thrown into the blaz-
ing furnace, the God we serve is able to save us from it, and He
will rescue us from your hand, O king. But even if He does not,
we want you to know, O king, that we will not serve your gods or
worship the image of gold you have set up."

We will not allow our circumstance to compromise our faith
in Christ Jesus!

Thank you and God Bless You,
Al and Yvette, LaTyia (Kyaime & Kyaime), Kimberly (Jesse &
Bobby), Kirkland, Tyler (Jessica), Trey, Culese, and Hannah

It seemed perfect. It was shortly thereafter that we began to encounter an explosion of loving and interested well-wishers, friends, and
family converging on us. Stephen Wilks (Alfred and Renita's eldest son)
and family were frequent visitors during this period. Their visits were
great and overwhelming at the same time! They loved being around
Yvette and she appreciated their loving affection. Yet their vitality reminded her constantly that she was sick and maybe dying. We tried to
find solace in it, but could not. Ultimately, we requested that visitors
give us a reprieve and asked Nana to stay with Yvette during the day.
She was starting to lose weight and her appetite was becoming mar-
ginal at best. One night, I sat on the couch with her, as she could no
longer sleep lying horizontally in bed. As I look back, I think we spent
most of the month of November sleeping on the couch. She asked me
a very direct question. "Babe, did the Lord tell you I was going to die?"

I looked at her, and I could not tell her what I knew, so I said, "I
had a dream, and in the dream you told me you were okay."

"That was it?" she replied. "Okay!"

She knew, and so did I. I leaned over and kissed her on the cheek and said, "This is so sad to me." That was all I could say. We cried together.

She told me, "Babe, it is going to be okay. Please stop!" I walked out of the family room into our bedroom and took a shower. The water from the shower almost concealed my tears. I got out of the shower and began to get my things ready for church the next day. It was November 21, 2009: the last night we would spend together in our home.

"With black folks, we find out what people were about in life from their obituary and **homegoing***. "*

—*President Barack Obama*

On Sunday, November 22, 2009, Lola had agreed to spend the morning with Yvette while we went to church. Yvette was unable to go to church any longer. She was always anxious to hear about the sermons and wondered what things she was missing while we were there without her. She would ask, "Hey, did anybody ask about me?" I'd always tell her "No." Of course, she knew that wasn't true. That morning we laughed together, and I thanked Lola for agreeing to stay with Yvette. Church service was pretty ordinary that day; most people who approached me would say, "I'm praying for you."

When I returned home, I remember walking in the door and looking at Lola's face. She was unsteady and pacing around Yvette, who was seated on the couch in her usual position breathing very rapidly. I remembered hearing the sound of the oxygen tank's hiss; it always made that sound when it was on maximum. I looked at Lola's face, and could tell immediately that she was concerned.

She came over and told me, "Yvette went to take a shower, and when she got out she said that she couldn't breathe. I've done everything I could think of to do!"

It was apparent Lola was on the brink of an emotional outburst.

I looked at Yvette's face again. She was breathing. You could see her chest rising and falling. She put four fingers up on one hand and on the other hand five...then one...then one...911. I looked at her and said, "You want me to call 911? Are you sure?" She nodded and didn't say anything. I sent Culese and Hannah into the back room, got on the telephone, and called 911. In the seven minutes that it took them to receive my call and send an ambulance to our home, Yvette had changed her mind.

"I don't want to go."

I looked at her, looked at Lola, looked back at her, and I said, "You are going. You don't look good. Your breathing is very rapid. I'm concerned." She stared back at me with that look of disapproval; Hannah always referred to the look as the "wide-eye." Yvette had the wide-eye on maximum. She did *not* want to go to the hospital and she did *not* want to be taken out of her home via ambulance. Some time ago we had made an agreement that, if she were close to passing away, we would try to arrange it so that she did not die at home. She did not want that to be part of her children's memory of their mom. Neither of us was thinking about our agreement in that moment, however. She had been to the emergency room many times in the last ten years. This was different, though. As the ambulance drove up I could hear the shrieking sirens. I went outside and waved at them; they stopped and walked into the house. After performing a couple of tests, the paramedics' eyes got big as saucers and they said, "Ma'am, are you okay? Can you hear us? Are you okay?"

She looked at them and she laughed. "I can hear you."

That's what she said. She said it again: "I can hear you!"

I laughed. She did not want to go to the hospital, but I said, "You are going." They put her on the gurney and were off to the hospital. I turned and Lola said, "I'll get the kids. We are fine. I'll stay here."

Off to the hospital I went. I remembered thinking while en route to Kaiser, *where is this going?* I prayed while I was driving, "God, Lord Jesus, help us!"

I arrived at the hospital moments after the ambulance. After I parked the car, I said another prayer and walked into the emergency room. I remember seeing a familiar face flash by me, as someone I knew was at the emergency room. I located the room that Yvette was in. It wasn't long before the doctor came back and said, "We have to take some X-rays. Your oxygen level is very low, ma'am." They took X-rays, and the results were very clear: Yvette's lung had collapsed again. The doctor came back in after looking at the X-rays. "We are going to insert a tube into the right part of your chest to reinflate your lung." I thought, *Insert a chest tube? How do you do that in the emergency room?* Well, shortly thereafter I would find out.

There was a flurry of people as doctors, nurses, and interns all gathered around Yvette. We were moved to a procedure room of sorts. I remember the doctor putting the Betadine fluid on Yvette's chest to clean the area. I was standing there. I had her bag, my bag, a sweat suit on, my jacket, her jacket, and sweat pants draped over me. I looked like a coat rack teetering on collapse. It was cold outside, and I was dressed for those conditions. No part of me was ready for the close confines of an overcrowded emergency-procedure room. I looked at Yvette as we were holding hands. The doctor suggested that we let go of our hands because they might need to stand on either side of her. I let go and stood back. One of the nurse interns looked at me and said, "Sir, are you okay?"

"I'm fine." But it was hot in there, and I was watching them. They began to poke a hole in my wife's chest. She sort of flinched her face and said, "Ouch!"

I began thinking, *I can't watch them do this to her.* I told them that I was going to leave the room. One of the nurses followed me out and gave me a glass of ice water. I took my hat off; I did not realize that my face was drenched in sweat. I remember thinking I had to go outside and get some air. I walked outside, and there was my oldest son waiting to ask me what happened. He had seen the ambulance pull off while he was in the Casita. I had forgotten that he was there. I walked out of the emergency room and I started crying. I spoke to the Lord in a way that I wish I hadn't. I asked God, "…what are You trying to do to me?" I couldn't take watching Yvette being poked at anymore. I prayed to God, asking that He make it me instead of her. "Take her out of this and put me in it!" I knew what was best, not Him. Later, I would apologize to God. I felt those words were so disrespectful, selfish, and rebellious. I sat down outside and waited several minutes, allowing my-self to calm down and cool off. I walked back in the procedure room; there was the chest tube coming out of Yvette's right side.

She was there smiling, wide awake, and said, "You know it didn't really hurt at all. They just poked it in...just like they said they would."

I shook my head and said, "You ready to go home?"

She looked at me. "Mr. Rowlett, I don't think I am going to be go-ing home like this."

Yeah, there was a chest tube draining fluid out of her right side. It would become part of the focus of our last thirteen days together. I said, "You are probably right." They assigned her to a room in the hospital and took her upstairs. I went up with her. I kissed her. I remember call-ing her sister, Pamela, to ask if she could spend the night with Yvette. Pamela wasn't working at that time and said, "Of course." It would be a standard part of my dialogue with Pam for the next thirteen days.

On Monday, November 23, 2009, our family began to accept and understand that Yvette was in the hospital and that it was quite serious. Yvette, on the other hand, was in an almost jovial mood. She had one thing on her mind. "I want you to get the retirement papers turned in, Mr. Rowlett, do you understand? And don't laugh!" She issued another edict. "I want you to go out and buy some new bedroom furniture for Hannah."

I said, "Say that again?"

"I want you to go out and buy some new bedroom furniture for Hannah."

I looked at her. She said, "Don't laugh at me."

I looked at her again. I wasn't laughing. I wondered if that chest tube had affected some other parts of her body, but I didn't argue. "I'll look at some new bedroom furniture for Hannah and certain-ly I will get the retirement papers turned in." Then we talked about Thanksgiving. She gave more very specific, strict instructions:

"Thanksgiving will be at LaTyia's house!"

I was not in a position to argue. Yvette had a chest tube inserted into her right side and was secured to the bed. She couldn't go anywhere, but she was in charge of this conversation. God, of course, has all the power, but on that day He transferred a little extra to her. I said, "Of course. Thanksgiving dinner will be at LaTyia's." I thought, *Maybe she'll be home by Thanksgiving. She seems so much better.* She was instructive, feisty…and yet…very focused on breathing and the chest tube.

On Tuesday, November 24, 2009, I had set up a plan for 24-hour staffing for my favorite patient, Yvette Rowlett. Friends and family supported me with putting together the schedule. I telephoned everyone: Bible-study sisters, mother, sister, and other buddies. Her sister, Pamela, was going to be with her during nocturnal shifts. A lot of people were on vacation, as it was close to Thanksgiving, and they were more than willing to come and spend some time with Yvette. Yvette was only slightly bothered by this as, unbeknownst to me at that time, she needed lots of nursing assistance and care with voiding. I told her it would be an honor and a privilege to help her go to the bathroom. She looked at me and tersely spoke, "Ha, ha, ha, Mr. Rowlett."

I came back with, "Nursing care, 24 hours a day for my favorite patient, that's my favorite job. I'm delighted to be your husband." I kissed her, machine-gun style, so many times she finally said, "Stop it, Babe, stop it!"

I told her that I had to talk to Hannah's teacher, to let her know what was going on and keep her informed as I didn't want to burden Hannah with trying to explain what was happening. I also said that I had called her father, and that he was coming out to see her. She was surprised and happy to hear he was coming to visit.

"Deddy is coming to see me? He doesn't have to do that."

I told her, "I think he wants to. He is going to come out for Thanksgiving and spend time with his daughter."

We spent Tuesday night together. Between Pam and me, we spent most of the next 13 nights with Yvette. She'd wake me up at night and apologize. "Babe, got to go…got to go, Babe."

I'd laugh. She'd say, "Sorry, Babe. Sorry."

And I'd say, "No problem, Mrs. Rowlett." She asked me constantly about the retirement papers. I assured her that I had turned them in to the California Personnel Retirement Office.

We had an unexpected visit on Tuesday from a surgeon, a Dr. Ryan Cox, who just so happened to be married to one of the EGUSD trustees. Small world! He was gracious, kind, informative, and frank. He explained that, while the small chest tube that they inserted in the ER was doing its job, it was insufficient to resolve the problems that Yvette had. He said that they would have to surgically insert a larger tube and try to reinflate her lung. We looked at each other and said, "Okay, surgical chest tube." The surgery was going to be scheduled sometime on Wednesday. We prayed. We asked God for His favor and His love. We thanked Christ Jesus for all the times that He had helped us and delivered us. We thanked God for the life He had given us, for the love that we would always have.

Coincidentally, Dr. Cox was one of the few people that Yvette trusted completely during those last 13 days. We would always feel better for a few minutes after Dr. Cox's visits. But, we were both beginning to wonder if she would ever come back home. She said,

"Remember, I do not want to die at home."

I kissed her. She kissed me.

"You promised. I don't want the kids to remember their mommy dying at home."

"I'll keep my promise. You won't die at home."

Tuesday, November 24, 2009, was the day Dr. Cox performed the surgical procedure. It didn't take place until very late that evening. I remember thinking, *Okay, let's see what happens.* Before surgery, he came by the waiting room area and he said, "Well, I am going to go and do what I can." Dr. Cox had an odd way of pausing; it was pleasant, and almost childlike. Lola was sitting in the family waiting area with us. I would hear her say, "We are praying for you as well, Dr. Cox." The surgery was completed, and afterwards Dr. Cox informed us that he was cautiously optimistic that it would work.

On Wednesday, November 25, 2009, the day before Thanksgiving, Deddy was in town. Pamela had picked him up from the airport and he was going to spend the day, the evening, and part of the next day with his daughter. I was introduced to *"palliative care."*

Yvette told me, "A nice lady from the hospital came by to see me. She's going to want to talk to you, Mr. Rowlett. Don't get upset. We talked about a lot of things. I'm prepared for what the Lord has for me, Mr. Rowlett. I don't want to leave you because you are really getting yourself together now, but if it means God can't use you, I'll leave and get out the way."

I looked at her when she said that. I was standing, and she was lying on the bed reciting this speech. I said, "If you don't want me to get upset, you shouldn't talk to me that way." She asked me again about the retirement papers. I said, "Everything has been turned in. It's all being completed. Now it is the matter of waiting to see what the Department of Education says about your retirement."

"Good job, Babe, good job!"

I was annoyed. Who was this person that needed to talk with me? As I was standing there, the lady from palliative care came in the room.

"I wanted to discuss durable power of attorney and the possibility that Yvette might die."

It was the first time that anyone at Kaiser had broached that subject with me, and I wasn't interested in having that conversation. I said, "Our God is able to heal her."

Yvette looked at me; then she looked at the lady and said, "He's not ready for that conversation yet."

I wasn't. I wasn't giving up. I was feeling guilty! I was feeling guilty about everything. I thought about my exit from the emergency room. I keep thinking that I just couldn't watch them poke Yvette. I've seen so many surgical procedures...but never hers. I was so irritated. Why did she talk with these people? Was she going to die?

I found solace in going to work (especially that day), as I could work for about three to four hours, returning to be with Yvette at her bedside. It was the new standard. The folks at the office were very supportive. I had sent out an e-mail to the employees explaining our circumstances and situation. Several of them wrote back, expressing their concern, and told me they were praying for us. I also found out that her brother, Jimmy, was coming to town, which was a very pleasant surprise. He was scheduled to arrive on Thanksgiving Day. When I returned to the hospital, Yvette's dad was sitting at her bedside. He had arrived a few hours earlier. I gave him a hug as he sat there with Yvette. I gave her a kiss, left the room, and let them spend that afternoon and evening together. It gave me a chance to attend to Hannah and Culese, and work on my part of Thanksgiving dinner. It was a difficult time, and it was the first time I felt alone. I wondered how Yvette felt. How many times she had felt alone? I thought about what the Lord said: "I will be with you always, even into the end of the earth." I hoped that was true.

Thanksgiving of 2009, the big distraction: it was Thanksgiving at my daughter's new home. Thanksgiving with the Rolles, and there was so much going on: Uncle Jimmy coming to town; Deddy, Yvette's father, leaving town; the girls visiting at the hospital; setting up more staffing for Yvette; and of course the discussions with Dr. Cox. All of those things occurred between Tuesday, November 24, and Saturday, November 28. Those days flew by like a supersonic jet; I cannot even remember eating Thanksgiving dinner. It was during that period that several visitors would stop by to see Yvette. Many of these visits were from the Bible-study sisters; they were focused on standing beside Yvette. They also worked shifts, as they were quite skilled at helping Yvette with the bedpan. They just felt it was their privilege, not duty, anything for their sister. She loved those ladies. I remember watching Yvette that Saturday night. Her breathing was not improving; it was getting worse.

Dr. Cox came by to visit Yvette; he candidly informed us, "…We are not getting the response we want from the chest tube."

I was concerned and disheartened, and so was he. Yet, Yvette and I never stopped praying and never gave up. Yvette was scared. For the first time in our life together, she was admittedly afraid of dying.

I told her, "…The Lord is going to allay our fears and we will rest in Him."

We would not talk about dying anymore; we would just look at each other.

All she said was, "Okay, Babe. Okay!"

The day after Thanksgiving is sometimes referred to as Black Friday; I called it Yvette's Retirement Friday! It was the day her retirement papers were filed and completed. The state offices were open that day. I assured Yvette that all was done. Yvette was pleased that the retirement papers were officially filed.

She looked at me and said, "Good job, Babe!"

Although she seemed pleased and relieved, she was so very tired. Her breathing was very labored at this point. The nurse came in and pointed out that some involuntary muscular responses had increased in the last few hours. The surgery to reinflate her lung obviously wasn't working. It was not a good time for either of us. The person from palliative care came by and gave us the options we dreaded. They were not good options. Prognosis: death was unavoidable. We prayed. We looked at each other a lot. She would not talk about coming home anymore. It was no longer a topic of conversation. We were focused only on staying alive and staying together.

The Bible-study sisters were making a tremendous impact on our lives with their support. Our Harvest Church family was actively praying, sending out messages via e-mail and letters, bringing food over, letting us know how much they loved us. We were seeking the Lord, as always. In our 28 years of marriage together, He had gotten us through the most difficult dilemmas; He would get us through this. No one knew it, but, between the two of us, we still believed that somehow God would make all of this right. We believed that one day we would look back on it as another major hurdle in our lives.

I decided on November 28th that I would sneak Hannah into the hospital. Getting Hannah into the hospital was actually quite humorous. They had changed Yvette's room at this point; she was now at the end of the hallway. I remembered throwing my jacket and another coat over Hannah's head, picking her up, and sticking her into the elevator. The H1N1 virus was the big concern at that time, and they did not want any children under the age of fifteen on the floors of the hospital with the patients. However, we were going to sneak Hannah in to see her mommy. The nurses colluded with us, and I snuck Hannah in, opened the door, closed it behind us, removed the jackets, and Hannah looked at her mom. I think that look told a lot. Hannah was afraid. She was horrified to see her mother hooked up to tubes, a breathing apparatus, IVs, and PIC lines.

Yvette sat up and said, "Hey Hannah!"

Hannah stopped, and she didn't say a word.

"Give Mommy a hug, big girl! Give Mommy a hug!" That's all Yvette said.

Hannah went over to the bed and gave her mother a hug. I said, "Hannah, it's okay. It's okay, Hannah."

Yvette looked at her and said, "I'm doing fine. I'm going to come home." Hannah laughed at that point, as she seemed to relax. Then she began to tell Yvette about school and about life; all the things that had been going on; all the things that Yvette missed.

"Thank you, Hannah! You are doing good? Take care of Daddy!"

Hannah looked at me as if that was an impossible task. Then I sort of whisked Hannah out of the room, deposited her in front of the TV in the waiting area, and went back in Yvette's room. I went over to the bed, and Yvette started to cry. That was a hard day. She didn't like the fact that Hannah saw her that way, and the way she reacted! Yvette knew she was very sick. She said, "I guess I scared her with all my stuff."

I said, "Well, the mind of an eight-year-old."

She didn't dare ask me, but I knew what she was thinking: Did I think she would be alive when Hannah turned nine years old?

Sunday, November 29, 2009, that day was filled with lots of doctors' visits. At some point the charge nurse finally came to the room and said, "Mr. Rowlett, I'm concerned. We are going to umm…umm…" She kept saying "umm."

"Mr. and Mrs. Rowlett, I think we should take you to the ICU."

"ICU?" I said.

"Well, her breathing continues to be very labored, and we are concerned."

She was talking very fast. I said, "Okay."

After a short wait Yvette was being wheeled off to ICU.

ICU staff quickly got accustomed to all her visitors and their curiosity. At one point on Monday there were twelve people in Yvette's ICU room—our kids, John from Turning Point, her mother, her sister, the pastor, the pastor's wife—everybody was in ICU. I think everybody sort of expected that Yvette would die in the ICU. On Monday, November 30, 2009, I spent the night in ICU. That night, something interesting happened. Yvette got a phone call from her brother. I know it was her brother because it was 11:00 p.m. and the caller was identified as Dr. Peters. I thought, *Dr. Peters?* Yvette knew immediately. She smiled and said, "I'll take the call." She was not talking, just listening. I remember the end of the telephone conversation; right before Yvette gave me the phone back she said, "I love you!" In all my years of marriage to Yvette, I had not heard her say it that way to her brother: "I love you!" It was the way she said it. Oh, it wasn't that she didn't love him! It was just simply not the way they interacted. They loved each other without having to say, "I love you." But that night she wanted him to know, "I love you!"

On Tuesday, December 1, 2009, they decided to move Yvette out of the ICU. Yvette was adamantly opposed to the plan. She said, "They are moving me out of the ICU so I can be in the hospital when I die."

"I don't think so."

"I know. I heard them."

I approached one of the nurses and said, "She thinks you are moving her out of ICU because she is going to die."

She replied, "Sir, there simply isn't anything that we can do for your wife in ICU."

I thought to myself, *They are moving my wife out of ICU because they think she is going to die and there is nothing that they can do.* Yvette looked at me and said, "See, I told you."

"Yvette, it's going to be okay." She didn't want to talk to me anymore. "Get Dr. Cox here!"

She didn't want to leave ICU. She was scared, and so was I. Dr. Cox and some of the other physicians were summoned. They came into the room and began to talk to me about comfort care. What a phrase for a disciple of Christ: "*comfort care!*" I wanted to say that our Lord is our comfort. In a time of our most desperate need, the Lord is our comfort. I thought "*comfort care*" meant no pain. They were wrong. I believed that God was going to heal her. That His grace and power, His mercy and love would transform Yvette's weak, sick, diseased body into a healthy body. And she would somehow miraculously walk out of that hospital room and say to the whole world, "…Look at me!" I had visions of her being on the *Oprah Winfrey Show* and saying, "Oprah, I was sick and dying and look at me now!" That was the vision I had. It didn't happen that day, but I knew that very soon God was going to heal her.

On Wednesday, December 2, 2009, Yvette was back on the fourth floor with a room in the middle of the hallway. Kind of a nice, quaint room, except it was very loud. There were several other individuals who had guards at the door of their rooms. I joked and said, "Yvette, do you want a security guard?" In between breaths she would say, "To help me breathe." We laughed. That was a day filled with laughter. That was a good day, but on that day Yvette became very, almost exclusively focused on her oxygen level, on her health indicators, and staying alive. She would ask me countless times, "What is the oxygen level, Babe?"

"Okay, I can't talk. I have to get it down." Every time she talked her heart rate would elevate and her oxygen level would drop down. She would look at the monitor, and after the readings returned to normal say, "See? Good job!"

She was fighting to stay alive.

I was focused on doing my part. I made a vow to her and to God, "You keep her alive, and I'll do everything else." I can remember sleeping at the hospital that night and waking up with throbbing pain in my back and in my ribs. It was cold, and I was uncomfortable. When I got up in the middle of the night, it felt like someone had stabbed me in the rib. "Babe, need to go to the bathroom."

She sounded like a little kid. And I could still laugh and say, "My pleasure, Miss!" I think that when the two become one flesh, you decide that it doesn't matter. You do whatever God gives you permission to do to care and sustain that person. I was committing to God and to her that I was going to do whatever I could. I would pick up her legs and slide the bedpan under her. She'd void, and then I would pick her legs back up and move it out. However, every time I would pick up her legs, her heart rate would increase and her breathing would become short and uncomfortable. The nurses decided to get her a catheter, and my job manning bedpans was over. Now, my job was to sit at her bedside and pray. When she slept, I cried and I prayed.

I believe that it is a privilege to sit beside someone that wants you to be there when they are preparing to go to heaven. I did not know that was what I was doing, that I was gazing at a miracle. I had no idea what was going to happen. Yvette truly was going to be transformed. I was so focused on the here and now. I wanted God to know that I was never going to give up.

On Thursday, December 3, 2009, Yvette was assigned to a new room in the corner. There was nobody next door to us. I did not appreciate it then, but now I know why they wanted Yvette in that room. It was because they were preparing for her to die. They didn't want the other patients who were getting well to experience that. When we went to that room in the corner I said, "Hey, you got the corner estate!" I was shocked back into reality when the nice lady from palliative care came by and she said, "Mr. Rowlett, the doctors are recommending that, when your wife is well enough, she go into a nursing home."

I looked at her and I said, "Go to a nursing home? Are you saying that she'll never come home again?"

"Mr. Rowlett, the doctors don't think that your wife will be coming home for a very long time."

All I could say was, "...That's very sad to me." I looked up to heaven and I looked at Yvette. *Am I dreaming? Is this a nightmare? Is this a bad dream? God could command the disease to go away; why won't he heal her?* I thought about what Elijah did when the woman came in and told him that her son was ill. How he lay out across her son and prayed, "…mouth to mouth and eye to eye." I thought about that and doing it with Yvette. I thought, *If I do that, I'll crush her and they'll arrest me.* I chuckled, and both of them stared at me. Yvette never spoke another complete sentence after that; she was focused on beating death. I sat there with her for hours; I didn't say anything. I just prayed.

Friday, December 4, 2009, that was our last day and night together. That day, people came in and out of the room. Yvette was just breathing. They would give her medications so she would not experience any pain. I wasn't opposed to comfort care. I simply didn't believe it was necessary. At one point I remember saying to folks, "Okay, no more visitors. She is tired. She needs to rest." The kids didn't come by anymore. I told them it was best if they stayed away. Their mom was very sick. They said, "Okay, Daddy." The day was quite forgettable, but that night was amazing. I told Pamela that I was going to spend the night at the hospital. I don't know why I picked Friday. I just did. I picked Friday. I decided that I would spend that night with her. Something happened during the evening; the respiratory therapist came into the room, knocked on the door, and wanted to give Yvette an oxygen treatment. I had shortly before that gotten on my knees and prayed. I had prayed in a way I had never before prayed in my life. I said, "Lord, if you aren't going to heal Yvette, please take her home." I didn't want Yvette to hear me. "Lord, if you aren't going to heal Yvette, please take her home." I wanted the Lord to know that I wasn't giving up but that I didn't want to see her suffer. The respiratory therapist came in and applied the breathing treatment. When she removed Yvette's oxygen mask, Yvette started fighting with her. I thought, what is Yvette trying to do? We pushed Yvette's arms down; she resisted. We had to force her to put that mask back on. She gave me a look that communicated, *Hmmm…I'll show you.* I'd seen the look before. I thought, *That's not a good sign.* She breathed all night long. She just looked at me. I would hold her hand until she went to sleep; she would wake up and just look at me. She didn't take the oxygen mask off again. What I know retrospectively is that she was trying to go home right then, but I didn't let her. That was our last night together.

First Thessalonians, chapter 4, verse 13 (NKJV): "But I do not want you to be ignorant, brethren, concerning those who have fallen asleep, less due sorrow as others who have no hope. For if we believe that Jesus died and rose again, even so, that will bring with him those who sleep in Jesus."

Saturday morning I decided Yvette was going to get better. Denial had pursued me all night and captured me. I was fully embracing it. I decided I was going to work. I'd scheduled the Bible-study sisters to relieve me first thing in the morning on Saturday. Two of them showed up to be with Yvette that morning. I greeted them, "I'm going to go to work now and I'll see Yvette later." As they went in, I looked at Renita and Lola, smiled again, and said, "Okay ladies, I'm going to work and I'll see you all later." They just kind of stared at me, perplexed, and then went to have fellowship and devotion with their sister. As I drove off to work, I decided while I was en route to give my daughters a call. They had encamped at the house and were taking care of Hannah and Culese. I called them and determined they were all doing okay. They said I needed to come home and wash Hannah's hair because someone was going to come to the house and braid it that day. I said, "Okay, I will, but I'm going to go to work first."

I arrived at the office and found everyone busily preparing for a monumental event. They were working on a training that was going to start on Monday: Immersion Training. Several people were there. I walked in and greeted everyone. They looked kind of glum and shocked. One of our managers from Modesto had driven to Sacramento that morning to get a quick overview, just in case there was an emergency with Yvette. I said, "Good, you're here! I think I'm going to be able to complete the Immersion Training, but I'm glad you're here." He looked at me and said, "Great, Al!" They all seemed a bit surprised. It was getting close to about 10:00 a.m., and I decided to walk outside and get some air. As I was walking outside, my cellular telephone rang. It was a doctor from Kaiser Hospital and she said, "Mr. Rowlett, where are you?"

"I'm at work!"

"Mr. Rowlett, your wife is dying."

I was not prepared to hear that. "What?"

"Mr. Rowlett, your wife is dying."

I paused and just responded, "Okay."

She said, "Come back to the hospital."

"Okay."

I walked around a small quad area that is adjacent to our administrative office. Tears were streaming down my face. Denial wasn't working any longer. Yvette was dying. I walked back into the office, looked at everybody, and I said, "Hey, guys, the doctor just called me and they told me that my wife is dying and I have to go back to the hospital." They didn't say anything, and I walked out.

1 Kings, chapter 9, verses 11–12 (NKJV): "Then He said, 'Go out, and stand on the mountain before the Lord.' And behold, the Lord passed by, and a great and strong wind tore into the mountains and broke the rocks in pieces before the Lord, but the Lord was not in the wind; and after the wind an earthquake, but the Lord was not in the earthquake; and after the earthquake a fire, but the Lord was not in the fire; and after the fire a still small voice."

As I got into the car I remember thinking, *I'm going to go home and kiss my girls first.* And then I heard a "still small voice" that was so clear and direct: "You need to go to the hospital!"

I looked up to God, and I said, "Go to the hospital? Okay! I'll go to the hospital." But I was going to drive by the house first. I was driving. I was rationalizing. Again the voice, it was very clear: "You need to go to the hospital!"

I called my girls and said, "Hey girls, the doctor called me. I have to go to the hospital." I remember the drive to the hospital, just thinking about everything that Yvette and I had done. All the years of work... all the years of prayer...all the years of learning from the Holy Spirit... and now the Holy Spirit was directing me to get back to the hospital. I arrived at the hospital, parked the car, and walked up to her room. I walked in her room as the Bible-study sisters were walking out. One of the Bible-study sisters commented, almost inquisitively, "You know she was trying to take that oxygen mask off?"

It had not dawned on me that Yvette had decided, "*Well, if he is not going to act right and let me die with him, I'll die with my sisters.*" Now, I'm sure that was what she was trying to do. I walked in the room and I tried to shut the door. As I was shutting the door, I felt a hand pushing the door back. "I just want to get a quick glimpse of her," the friend said.

I said, "No!"

"Just one quick glimpse?"

She stuck her head inside the door and said, "That's all I need. Bye, honey!"

I recalled Yvette had visited her sister years earlier after she had contracted cancer, had a stroke, and later died. She left and I shut the door and I looked at Yvette. I wasn't sure she was aware that I was there. I sat on a chair and leaned back. "Being comfortable," I said, just like a man refusing to relinquish control of his life. "Lord, if you are not going to heal her body, please take her home."

I heard the "still small voice" say, "You don't pray like that, sitting in a chair. You better get on your knees, servant." I was stunned. I got on my knees next to Yvette's bed and I began to pray, "Lord, God... Dear Lord Jesus, if you are not going to heal her body, please take her home." I remember standing up and gazing around. I looked at Yvette and I looked at the room. Something had happened. Things were altered; it was different. Then I heard the "the still small voice" again: "Call her sister."

I got on the phone and I called her sister. I said, "Hey Pam, where are you?"

"I'm right here!"

"No...no...where are you?"

"I'm right here." Within an instant, she walked in the room. I was surprised. "You're here?"

"Yeah, I spent the night in the hospital."

I contradicted her. "No, I spent the night in the hospital."

"So did I! But when you told me you didn't need me to do the graveyard shift, well, I was already here; so I slept on the couch in the waiting area."

"I didn't know that." Then I looked at her. She had on the wildest outfit I'd ever seen. I asked her where she had been.

She said, "It's a long story."

Then we looked at Yvette and stopped talking...she was breathing very rapidly. Then I heard the "still small voice" again say, "Call her mother."

I said, "Call her mother?" "Call her mother!" Pam just stared at me; I am sure she was wondering "who was I conversing with." The Holy Spirit was directing everything. I picked up the phone again and called Nana.

"Hello Nana, this is Alfred."

"Hi Alfred."

I didn't mince words. "Hey, something is happening. You need to come to the hospital." Nana told me she would be up there at 3:00 that day. "Okay, but something is happening, and I don't know what it is."

There was a pause. "I'll be up there in 20 minutes."

I'm confident that Pamela and I did not speak for the next 20 to 30 minutes until Yvette's mother arrived. Nana arrived, stood on the right side of the bed, Yvette's right side, where the chest tube was draining fluid into a container. I stood on Yvette's left side, and Pamela stood at the end of the bed. We all just stood there, talking to Yvette, looking at each other and then back at Yvette. The nurse came into the room and gave her some medication in the IV for pain. She walked out, shutting the door. I kept looking at Yvette. So did her mother. After a few minutes, something amazing happened. Yvette took the oxygen mask off, almost wildly, with her hands. Her mother and I quickly realized that without her mask she couldn't breathe. We immediately grabbed it and tried to put it back on. Yvette, the lady who had not spoken for over a day, with those eyes so big and beautiful, stared at me. I stopped trying to put it back on. I could see her mother still trying to get the mask back on, but I stopped helping. Yvette looked at me and she spoke, in the weakest, most beautiful voice, "No."

It was the most glorious "*No*" I had ever heard. I looked at her, and again she said, "No."

I watched as her mother valiantly tried to get the mask back on. I gazed at her weak, frail body, and I knew. I spoke the words that only a husband who loves Christ Jesus and His gift, my **wife** for 28 years, should ever speak. I looked at her mother and said what the Spirit of God put in my mouth to speak: "Stop! Leave her alone."

Nana looked at me and put the mask down. Then suddenly Yvette started to breathe. She started to breathe the most desperate, most beautiful breaths I'd ever heard (1...2...3...4). Her mother started to cry out, "Oh, my baby... my baby... my baby!" Giant tears came down my face. All I could say was, "Yvette, you're going to die. Hey, you are going home." I grabbed as much of her as I could and I prayed to God (5...6...7). I said, "Lord, you tell her that I love her and I will never let her go; I will always remember her." She breathed those desperate breaths (8...9...10...11...). As she breathed, I'd stomp my foot on the ground. And I could hear the Holy Spirit saying, "You are stomping on death. It has no place in this room. Yvette is not dying; she is going home" (12). Then, suddenly, Yvette blew away and went home. I could hear her mother saying, "My baby! My baby just died!" Pamela hadn't spoken. She seemed stunned. I remember touching Yvette's arm in shock; all I said was, "Did you die? Did you die?" I knew the truth.

First Thessalonians, chapter 4, verse 15 (NKJV): "For this we say to you by the word of the Lord, that we who are alive and remain until the coming of the Lord, will by no means precede those who are asleep. For the Lord himself will be sent from heaven, with the shout, with the voice of the archangel and with the trumpet of God, and the dead in Christ will rise first. Then we who are alive and remain shall be caught up together with them in the clouds to meet the Lord in the air. And thus we shall always be with the Lord."

One day, Yvette, I will see you again because right now you are at Home with the Lord.

Epilogue

Babe's Prayer

"Dear Lord,

I thank You and praise You in Christ Jesus' name. I honor You, God, I do, and I will always honor You! I thank You for the twenty-eight years You gave Yvette and me; please tell her that I still miss the sound of "Babe, you okay?" when she would come in to the room, the smell of cocoa butter at night, her playful gestures and cold feet prior to falling asleep. Tell her I made several mistakes beginning forty days after she passed away, as I arrogantly tried to live my life without waiting on You. That in spite of it all, You continued to take care of me and provide for my every need.

"Finally, I relented and gave control of my life to You and began to grieve. Through all my mistakes, You never let me go and I have learned to be honest with You. I can now admit that I was scared and alone! That You taught me to share my fears with other brothers in the faith, my sad days, guilt, and pain. Just as Yvette had done for years with her Bible-study sisters, You taught me how to reach out and trust others when I needed to.

"Please tell her friendships have faded, marriages have ended, an election was lost and brother died; and, in spite of all this,

You keep teaching me how to be courageous the same way she was prior to going home. That You have taught me to be a better parent and friend as, "Your Word is a lamp for my feet, a light on my path" (Psalms 119:105 NIV), comforting me when I am in need. Because of You today I am truly blessed, as I have seen a little girl become a young lady and gone into the birthing room to watch our first grandchild being born. I have seen sons and daughters become close friends, struggling through disappointments and trusting You to help them overcome their fears. And, that You have equipped me to give of myself when there are others in need.

"Lord, I am so thankful that You brought Yvette into my life; please tell her I said hello, and that I will never forget her. I love You, Lord, I do, and I will always praise and love You,

Your servant!"

CPSIA information can be obtained at www.ICGtesting.com
Printed in the USA
BVOW05s2208161114

375209BV00001B/47/P

9 781478 728573